POCKET

STOCKHOLM

TOP EXPERIENCES · LOCAL LIFE

T0018196

CHARLES RAWLINGS-WAY, BECKY OHLSEN

Contents

Plan Your Trip 4

Stortorget square (p39)
DIMBAR76/SHUTTERSTOCK ©

COVID-19

We have re-checked every business in this book to ensure that it is still open after the COVID-19 outbreak. However, the economic and social impacts of COVID-19 will continue to be felt long after the outbreak has been contained, and many businesses, services and events referenced in this guide may experience ongoing restrictions. Some businesses may be temporarily closed, have changed their opening hours and services, or require bookings; some unfortunately could have closed permanently. We suggest you check with venues before visiting for the latest information.

Stockholm's Top Experiences

ANDREY SHCHERBUKHIN/SHUTTERSTOCK ©

Explore in the open air at Skansen (p64)

Study a shipwreck at Vasamuseet (p68)

Visit the royal residence at Drottningholm (p122)

KALIN EFTIMOV/SHUTTERSTOCK ©

TORYPHOTOS/SHUTTERSTOCK ©

Get on the water in the Archipelago (p134)

Tour the royal palace, Kungliga Slottet (p34)

Enter the world of Carl Milles at Millesgården (p108)

Get to know the Vikings at Historiska Museet (p98)

JONATHAN SMITH/LONELY PLANET ©

KIEVVICTOR/SHUTTERSTOCK ©
SCULPTURE 'THE FANTASTIC PARADISE' BY NIKI DE SAINT PHALLE AND JEAN TINGUELY

Admire modern art at Moderna Museet (p70)

Appreciate photography at Fotografiska (p82)

Tour the mighty Stadshuset (p114)

Dining Out

Stockholm is a city of food obsessions. The relatively small city has more than half a dozen Michelin-starred restaurants, with new and exciting places opening constantly, serving everything from veggie-minded superfoods to fast-food fads like the indefatigable burger. It's not unusual for people to plan their visits here around restaurant menus.

Daily Dining

If you don't plan on daily five-star dining, Stockholm's cafes offer a good range of salads, sandwiches etc. Vegetarians and the health-conscious are in luck, too, thanks to the recent explosion of 'green' restaurants serving nourishing superfood bowls of fresh produce and grains. At the other end of the spectrum, the city is currently obsessed with cheeseburgers.

Street Snacks

In the world of Swedish street food, hot dogs reign supreme

– the basic model is called a *grillad korv med bröd* (hot dog in a bun), although you can also ask for it boiled (*kokt*). Adventurous souls can request myriad different things done to their *korv*, chiefly involving rolling it up in flatbread with accompaniments from shrimp salad to mashed potatoes.

Festive Flavours

Around Christmas, many restaurants offer a *julbord*, a particularly gluttonous version of Sweden's world-famous smörgåsbord buffet. Among the usual delicacies of

herring, gravlax, meatballs, short ribs and blood pudding are seasonal gems like *Janssons frestelse*, a casserole of sweet cream, potato, onion and anchovy.

Best Restaurants

Kryp In An intimate, excellent dining spot that's upmarket without pretension. (p44)

Rosendals Trädgårdskafe Enjoy gorgeous produce in the midst of Djurgården botanical splendour. (p79)

Hermans Trädgårdscafé Top-flight vegetarian buffet with wide-open views. (p88)

Grands Verandan Best place in town to launch into

MICHELMOND/SHUTTERSTOCK ©

a classic Swedish smörgåsbord. (p57)

Woodstockholm New twists on traditional dishes, plus a wine bar. (p88)

Ekstedt Reindeer and pike-perch cooked in a wood-fired oven – what's not to like? (p105)

Best Vegetarian

Hermitage A fantastic veggie buffet in Gamla Stan. (p44)

Holy Greens A super-healthy take on fast food: delicious bowls of super-foods and proteins. (p57)

Mahalo Healthy bowls of greens, grains and trendy good-for-you things. (p90)

Chutney Heaping plates of vegetarian curries and stews in Södermalm. (p89)

Rutabaga Artful veggie delights from celebrity chef Mathias Dahlgren. (p55)

Best Swedish

Magnus Ladulås Swedish classics served in a medieval Gamla Stan setting. (p45)

Fem Små Hus A perfect combination of authentic

historical setting and traditional cuisine. (p45)

Pelikan An old-school Swedish beer hall with a solid menu of classics. If you haven't tried herring or reindeer yet, here's your chance. (p89)

Sturekatten Sip coffee or tea with cakes at this adorable old-school Östermalm cafe. (p106)

Top Tips

○ The weekday lunch special called *dagens rätt* is great value. It's a set menu served between 11am and 2pm, including a hot main dish, salad, drink, bread and coffee.

○ Many vegetarian eateries are also all-you-can-eat buffets, which are popular with locals.

○ For Swedish *husmanskost* (home cooking), head to old-school pubs and trad restaurants.

Bar Open

Nightlife in Stockholm ranges from a quiet pint in an underground cellar to a neon-lit club that only gets kicking around 3am. If you plan to hit the late-night clubs, it's important to check the website and put your name on the guest list. Dress to the nines and follow your instincts – or follow the crowd – and you're bound to find a good time.

JONATHAN SMITH/LONELY PLANET ©

Best Clubs & Bars

Akkurat A great Södermalm beer bar, with mussels on the menu. (p91)

Berns Salonger Fancy, well-designed space with loads of history. Live music and DJs. (p58; pictured)

Café Opera Rock stars cavort in one of the loveliest interiors in Stockholm. (p58)

East Good sushi and great cocktails at this Stureplan hang-out. (p59)

Kvarnen Traditional Södermalm beer hall with a popular late-night dance space. (p90)

Sturecompagniet The relatively low-key option in Stureplan, in a pretty, baroque space. (p106)

Lemon Bar Friendly Kungsholmen cocktail bar where late-night dancing is a very real possibility. (p118)

Solidaritet A Norrmalm dance club hosting electronic music and international DJs. (p59)

Debaser Strand Cool and friendly Södermalm bar with regular live music, at Hornstull beach. (p91)

Spy Bar A famously difficult club to get into, unless you're famous (or at least look like you are). (p106)

Top Tips

○ Coat checks are mandatory in many clubs and bars. There's usually a small fee (20kr to 30kr).

○ On popular nights, clubs may also charge a fairly hefty admission fee (150kr to 200kr) – and make you wait in line (unless you've managed to get yourself on the guest list).

○ Some clubs stay open later than the tunnelbana runs. Budget for a taxi.

Live Music

JONATHAN SMITH/LONELY PLANET ©

On any night in Stockholm you can catch emerging indie acts, edgy rock, blues and Balkan pop. Jazz has a particularly strong presence, with several legendary venues saxing it up and an annual jazz festival in October. Classical concerts can be surprisingly affordable, and big names in rock and pop music tour through the city regularly.

Jazz

Swedish jazz has been going strong since the 1930s, and peaked in the '50s with artists such as Lars Gullin and Monica Zetterlund. Live jazz clubs are popular; the annual **Stockholm Jazz Festival** (www.stockholmjazz.com; ticket price varies by venue; ☺Oct) is mandatory listening.

Rock & Pop

Everyone knows about ABBA of course, and fans can check out their museum (p76)...but there's a lot more to Swedish pop than Agnetha, Björn, Benny and Frida. Sweden is the third-largest exporter of music in the world, behind the US and UK, remarkable when you consider the size of the population.

Opera & Classical

There's no shortage of live experiences in the classical or operatic realms here, either. The Stockholm opera house is a national landmark, while the classical Konserthuset is both affordable and accessible.

Best Jazz & Rock

Glenn Miller Café Jazz and blues bar with a devoted crowd of regulars. (p60)

Debaser Strand Indie rock and mainstream acts. (p91)

Mosebacke Etablissement Big-name live bands and local faves. (p92)

Stampen Homey jazz and blues joint. (p47)

Fasching Premier jazz club, weekend DJs. (p59; pictured)

Best Opera & Classical

Konserthuset Classical concerts are held in this elegant blue building. (p60)

Operan The royal opera house – any visit here is an experience. (p59)

Treasure Hunt

Shopping is a sport, a pleasure and an art form in Stockholm. Whether you're just browsing or looking for specific gifts to bring home, there are plenty of options spread across the various neighbourhoods. Even when it's cold and dark outside, the city's terrific malls and department stores don't miss a commercial beat.

JONATHAN SMITH/LONELY PLANET ©

What to Buy

Quintessentially Swedish things to bring home as gifts and souvenirs include hand-carved wooden toys and figures, such as the famous painted Dalahäst figures; glass and crystal, both decorative and utilitarian; fine linens and textiles; and intricate Sami handicrafts, especially leather, woodwork and jewellery made of woven metal threads.

Where to Shop

For big-name Swedish and international retail outlets and high-end boutiques,
hit the pedestrianised Biblioteksgatan from Östermalm to Norrmalmstorg, as well as the smaller streets that branch off it.

For funkier, artier and secondhand stores and galleries, head to Södermalm. And for classic souvenirs, T-shirts and postcards, check out picturesque Gamla Stan.

Best Big Stores

NK Huge department store with upscale souvenirs. (p60)

Åhléns Excellent department store with multiple locations. (p60)

Mood Stockholm Hip, stylish shopping centre. (p61)

Västermalmsgallerian Busy mall at the Fridhemsplan tunnelbana stop. (p121)

PK Huset A very central shopping mall, big on Swedish brands. (p61)

Top Tips

On most major purchases, depending on where you live, you can reclaim your sales tax at customs when departing Sweden. Keep your receipts and ask for a tax-free form from the vendor.

Fashion

MASKOT/GETTY IMAGES ©

Stockholm is Sweden's (some say Scandinavia's) fashion hub, and a major producer and exporter of emerging design talent. The big shopping districts are also home to just about every imaginable international design name, from Stella McCartney to Louis Vuitton. There are also fabulous secondhand and vintage shops across the city.

Sustainability

Perhaps unsurprisingly in a country as green as Sweden, sustainability is a big issue in fashion. Several Swedish brands place an emphasis on keeping their manufacturing processes eco-friendly and ethical. Check out the **Sustainable Fashion Academy** (www.sustainablefashionacademy.org).

Best Modern Fashion

Acne Skinny jeans and impeccable cool, now world-famous. (p51)

Marimekko Wild, playful patterns on everything from frocks to handbags and kitchen gadgets. (p51)

Filippa K Dead-serious design for grown-ups. (p51)

Whyred Understated and street-smart clothing inspired by musicians. (p51)

BLK DNM A new venture from the sketchbook of J Lindeberg. (p51)

WESC Skater-inspired fashion and gear, marketed worldwide by the rich and famous. (p51)

Best Vintage

59 Vintage Store High-quality retro clothing from the '50s through to the '70s. (p118)

Judits Famously well-curated vintage clothing. (p93)

Lisa Larsson Second Hand Cool secondhand clothes in a fun shop. (p93)

Smiley Vintage Remade styles from vintage clothing. (p93)

Top Tips

Stockholm Street Style (www.stockholm-streetstyle.com) Street fashion blog.

Stockholm Fashion Week (www.stockholmfashionweek.com) Sets the catwalks abuzz every autumn.

Design

Scandinavia is famous for ahead-of-its-time design, and there's plenty to be found around Stockholm. The city is all about good design, merging form and function in a relatively democratic – or at least ubiquitous – way. Bring samples of it back home with you, be inspired by how it's used, or just admire Scandistyle in its native environment.

JONATHAN SMITH/LONELY PLANET ©

Best Design

Svenskt Tenn The Josef Frank–led school of design still holds sway over the city. (p107)

Nordiska Galleriet A store that doubles as a showroom and design-freak nirvana. A dizzying array of nifty things. (p107)

Iris Hantverk Clever and beautifully made household items. (p51)

Nationalmuseum The largest collection of Swedish design objects can be found at the national art gallery. (p54; pictured)

Filippa K One of Sweden's groundbreaking early designers has shops in several locations around town. (p51)

DesignTorget This chain of accessible but cutting-edge design (household goods, gadgets etc) has several central locations. (p93)

NK This department store has a fantastic selection of quintessentially Swedish design products, from serving trays to tea towels and candle holders. (p60)

Marimekko Finnish design known for bold prints on textiles and dishes. (p51)

Café Opera Join the jet-set at this glitzy Norrmalm venue, revamped by Thomas Sandell. (p58)

Sturehof Popular high-end seafood restaurant and bar in Östermalm, designed by Jonas Bohlin. (p105)

Top Tips

For a new-design twist on the traditional Swedish wooden horses (Dalahäst), look into the work of Kerstin Oldal (www.kerstin oldal.com), who reinterprets the national symbol in gorgeous ways.

Architecture

PAWEL SZCZEPANSKI/SHUTTERSTOCK ©

Stockholm has a well-preserved cache of buildings from various important eras of architecture. For a good overview of Swedish architecture and its various lineages, as well as quick primers on current movements, stop in at ArkDes (p78). And don't miss **Globen** *(www.stockholmlive.com), the kooky giant golf-ball entertainment venue.*

Early Styles

Most of Stockholm's notable buildings are premodernist – the two royal palaces, Kungliga Slottet and Drottningholm, for example, and the imposing Stadshuset. A fairly brief but noteworthy period in regional architecture was Swedish National Romanticism – an often decorative classical free-style with Arts and Crafts influences, also known as Jugendstil.

Names to Drop

Erik Gunnar Asplund (1885–1940) is argu-
ably Sweden's most important modern architect. He's responsible for the iconic Stadsbiblioteket as well as the stunning Skogskyrkogården cemetery. Another name you'll hear frequently is Peter Celsing, who designed the stubbornly contemporary Kulturhuset. Many of the most important buildings in Stockholm were designed by the court architect Nicodemus Tessin the Elder. Tessin the Younger designed the 'new' Kungliga Slottet and worked on several other standout buildings.

Best Buildings

Stadsbiblioteket A graceful building, anyway you look at it. (p129)

Kulturhuset The design of this 1974 arts centre pushes the envelope, and divides architectural tastes. (p54)

Dramaten The Royal Dramatic Theatre is a decadent example of Jugendstil glory. (p107; pictured)

Stadshuset The City Hall is sturdy and square on the outside, secretly glittering within. (p114)

Östermalms Saluhall A many-spired cathedral of gourmet food, delectable both inside and out. (p105)

Museums & Galleries

Stockholm does museums properly – there's really not a bad one in the bunch. Maybe it's a perk of having a design-obsessed culture – whatever the reason, this city makes learning fun. Its art galleries are intensely stylish, the kind of places you want to dress up for, and its history museums employ multimedia to engage and enthral you (and the kids).

MANUEL VELASCO/GETTY IMAGES ©

Best Museums

Kungliga Slottet The royal palace contains a number of museums and is itself a masterpiece – it's the world's largest royal castle, still used for its original purpose. (p34)

Skansen An open-air museum of Swedish history and culture. Plan on spending at least a day exploring. (p64)

Vasamuseet Purpose-built museum devoted to the story of the ill-fated warship *Vasa*, which sank to the bottom of the sea in 1628. (p68)

Historiska Museet Engrossing multimedia presentation of the country's culture and history, arcing across 10,000 years. (p98)

Nobelmuseet Be inspired by stories of the most creative people of our time – recipients of the Nobel Prize. (p42)

Medeltidsmuseet Take the kids on a time-travelling tour of medieval Stockholm and the underpinnings of the royal palace. (p42)

Nordiska Museet Swedish art and artefacts through the ages, entertainingly arranged. (p75; pictured)

Spritmuseum A fun look at the complicated relationship Sweden has with alcohol. And there are tastings! (p75)

Tekniska Museet Kids of all ages will be fascinated by seeing how stuff works. Interactivity is the name of the game: push, pull, prod, measure and test. (p111)

Nationalmuseum It's big! The nation's largest collection of arts, across the ages. (p54)

Best Galleries

Moderna Museet One of the best places in Europe to check out some astounding modern art. (p70)

Fotografiska Go snap-happy at this stylish Södermalm photographic museum/gallery. (p82)

Bonniers Konsthall Cutting-edge art in a cutting-edge building in Vasastan. (p129)

Prins Eugens Waldemarsudde An excellent Nordic art gallery in a beautiful waterside location. (p77)

For Kids

Stockholm is well set up for travelling with children. There are baby-changing tables in almost every public bathroom, and even top-end restaurants have high chairs and children's menus. Likewise, hotel and hostel staff are accustomed to catering to families. On top of that, many museums offer free admission to children under 18 (sometimes older).

TRABANTOS/SHUTTERSTOCK ©

Best Kid-Friendly Sights

Junibacken Draws young readers into Swedish author Astrid Lindgren's fantastic world, home to Pippi Longstocking and her friends. (p76)

Naturhistoriska Riksmuseet Offers an interactive child's-eye view of the natural world (stuffed things, preserved things, exhumed things), with an entire section for hands-on science experiments. (p104)

Medeltidsmuseet Provides multimedia displays that transport visitors back in time to the city's earliest days. Under a bridge in Gamla Stan. (p42)

Gröna Lund Tivoli It's cheesy, but the carnival-ride entertainment here is always a hit with slightly older kids and teens. (p78; pictured)

Tekniska Museet Interactive science exhibits will entertain inquisitive brains for hours. (p111)

Skansen Essentially a younger child's paradise, with dozens of mini exhibits to explore, snacks everywhere, a zoo, singalongs and guides in old-timey costumes. (p64)

Nobelmuseet Has a 'Children's Club' (Barnens Nobelklubb) where kids aged between seven and 10 can share ideas and create. (p42)

Spårvägsmuseet Play tunnelbana driver and see how the excellent Stockholm transit system came to be. (p88)

Leksaksmuseet Toys of all kinds cram the shelves at this out-of-the-way museum. (p88)

Top Tips

Even if they aren't particularly geared towards children, most of Stockholm's museums have family playrooms available.

Parks

OLASER/GETTY IMAGES ©

Beautiful parks are a dime a dozen in Stockholm; you can hardly turn a corner without finding one. Most have good places for a picnic, nice benches and sturdy playground equipment for kids. Some also have lakes or beaches for swimming, good hiking trails and sometimes even small cafes for refreshments. Make like the locals and enjoy!

Picnics

Many casual cafes and coffee shops will offer breakfast or lunch 'packets', which make excellent-value picnic fixings. You can also pick up supplies in the prepared food section of many supermarkets, or in department stores such as NK (p60), whose high-end grocery section has the makings of a luxurious picnic.

Beaches

You're allowed to swim from just about any place where you can elbow your way into the water, but some swimming areas are nicer than others. Ask around – lots of locals have secret favourites among the city's beaches – or head to the Stockholm Archipelago or the water's edge near Rålambshovsparken.

Royal Parks

Some city parks have a royal lineage, notably Djurgården, both established and administered by various Swedish kings. They're now open to the public and are excellent places for running, walking or cycling (...don't worry, you're unlikely to encounter a deer-hunting king these days).

Best Parks

Djurgården The historical royal game park, established in the 15th century.

Vasaparken Lovely oasis in the middle of Vasastan.

Humlegården Home of the royal library in Östermalm, and a peaceful hang-out in its own right (pictured).

Rålambshovsparken This park abuts an excellent public swimming beach in Kungsholmen. (p117)

Ladugårdsgärdet Wide-open parklands just east of Östermalm.

Tantolunden Stay fit in Södermalm with an outdoor gym and waterside trails. (p88)

LGBTIQ+

Stockholm is a dazzling spot for queer travellers. Sweden's legendary open-mindedness makes homophobic attitudes rare, and party-goers of all persuasions are welcome in any bar or club. As a result, Stockholm doesn't really have a gay district, although you'll find most of the queer-centric venues in Södermalm and Gamla Stan.

STEFAN HOLM/SHUTTERSTOCK ©

Best Bars & Clubs

Lady Patricia (📞08-743 05 70; www.patricia.st; Söder Mälarstrand, Kajplats 19; ⏰5pm-midnight Wed & Thu, to 5am Fri-Sun; 🚇Slussen) Half-price seafood, nonstop dance music and decks packed with sexy Swedes and drag queens make this former royal yacht a gay Sunday night ritual (though you can now visit five nights a week). Head to the upper dance floor (past the pirates in the riggings) where lager-happy punters sing along to Swedish Eurovision entries with a bemusing lack of irony.

Side Track (📞08-641 16 88; www.sidetrack. nu; Wollmar Yxkullsgatan 7; ⏰6pm-1am Wed-Sat;

🚇Mariatorget) Claiming the title of Stockholm's oldest gay bar, this establishment in Södermalm has a low-key, publike ambience and decent bar food (fish and chips, curry, quesadillas). Check online for a schedule of theme nights and events.

Top Tips

o The national organisation for LGBTIQ+ rights is **Riksförbundet för Sexuellt Likaberättigande** (RFSL; 📞08-50 16 29 00; www.rfsl.se; Alsnögatan 7, Danvikstull; ⏰10am-noon & 1-3pm Mon & Wed-Fri; 🚌53, 71, 93, 402).

o For club listings and events, pick up a free copy of the magazine *QX* (www.qx.se).

o *QX* also produces a free, handy *Gay Stockholm Map*, available at the tourist office.

o The annual **Stockholm Pride** (www.stockholmpride.org; ⏰late Jul/early Aug; pictured) celebration happens between late July and early August.

For Free

KERT/SHUTTERSTOCK ©

Short on cash? Check museum schedules for free nights – most of them have one or two per week. Public parks and beaches are a handy way to fill a budget afternoon, as is window-shopping in Norrmalm, people-watching in Södermalm or wandering through park-studded neighbourhoods like Djurgården or Gärdet.

Best Free Stuff

Stadshuset Swimming at City Hall is free, if you've got the gumption to dive from the terrace with the locals. (p114)

Rålambshovsparken Swim, play, picnic or just hang out with an airport novel in this large park in Kungsholmen. (p117)

Moderna Museet Free admission! Modern art! It's a winning combination and Stockholm's most challenging art museum. (p70)

Stampen Every Sunday afternoon around 2pm, the regular Stampen crowd gets busy with a blues jam. (p47)

Tekniska Museet From 5pm to 8pm Wednesday, bring the whole family in to roam

this huge, fun technology museum for free. (p111)

Kulturhuset There are plenty of free kids' activities at this arts hub, from hands-on crafts to a comic-book library. (p54)

Riksdagshuset Take an engaging free tour of the Swedish Parliament building in Gamla Stan. (p43)

Royal Armoury Check out the amazing old suits of armour and sundry scary weapons beneath the Royal Palace. (p42)

Medeltidsmuseet Delve into medieval Stockholm at this free museum, beneath a bridge between Norrmalm and Gamla Stan. (p42)

Mårten Trotzigs Gränd It won't cost you one red cent

to traverse Stockholm's skinniest street. (p44; pictured)

Hallwylska Museet Who said hoarding was a bad thing? This amazing museum in Norrmalm offers a window into a *serious* collector's soul. (p54)

Armémuseum If you need convincing that war isn't the best way for people to spend their time, this free Östermalm museum will do the trick. (p104)

Sergels Torg Hang out in Norrmalm's hyperactive central square and watch the hum of humanity (...actually, it's more circular than square). (p55)

Festivals & Events

There's nearly always something going on in Stockholm, especially during the summer months. Whether you're interested in grazing the offerings of some of the city's best restaurants, sampling some international music or film, or just exploring whatever's on the seasonal activity menu, you're likely to find something of interest.

ARTESIA WELLS/SHUTTERSTOCK ©

Best in Summer

Midsummer Arguably the most important Swedish holiday, Midsummer's Eve traditionally falls on the Friday between 19 and 25 June; revellers head to the countryside to raise the maypole (pictured), sing and dance, drink and eat pickled herring (Midsummer Day is usually spent recovering).

Smaka På Stockholm A five-day celebration of Stockholm food. The program includes gourmet food stalls (including representatives from several archipelago restaurants), cooking demos and entertainment on Kungsträdgården. It's free to get in, and food offerings tend to be good value.

Stockholm Pride This annual parade and festival is dedicated to creating an atmosphere of freedom and support for gay, lesbian, bisexual and transgender people. It's one of the most exuberant pride festivals in Europe.

Best in Autumn & Winter

Stockholm Jazz Festival One of Europe's premier jazz festivals happens every October. (p13)

Stockholm International Film Festival Screenings of new independent films, director talks and discussion panels draw cinephiles to this important festival; tickets go quickly, so book early if you're interested. The ticket office is in Kulturhuset. (p54)

Gamla Stan Christmas Market (www.stortorgets julmarknad.com) Usually opening in mid-November, this adorable Stockholm market in Gamla Stan's main square (Stortorget) can almost single-handedly lift the spirits on a cold winter night. Shop for handicrafts and delicacies, or just wander with a mug of cocoa and a saffron bun.

Four Perfect Days

Day One

ADAM GRINSHAW/LONELY PLANET ©

Start early and beat the crowds to Gamla Stan. Fortify yourself with a coffee and pastry, then tour the royal palace, **Kungliga Slottet** (p34). Allow two or three hours to see everything.

For lunch, head for the buffet at **Hermitage** (p44; pictured). Walk it off with a stroll from Gamla Stan across Norrbro and along the water's edge to the footbridge that crosses to the island of Skeppsholmen. Here you can visit **Moderna Museet** (p70), then stop in for something completely different – 1000 years of Swedish architecture on display next door at **ArkDes** (p78).

After, walk back over the footbridge and into Norrmalm for a drink at **Berns Salonger** (p58). For dinner, make your way to **Grands Verandan** (p57) for the famous Swedish smörgåsbord.

Day Two

MINO SURKALA/SHUTTERSTOCK

On your second day, spend a few hours exploring **Skansen** (p64) – 'Sweden in miniature'. Be sure to see the animals at the Nordic zoo, and don't miss the glassblowers' cottage.

Venture on to Djurgården for lunch at **Rosendals Trädgård-skafe** (p79), then backtrack to the **Vasamuseet** (p68) dedicated to the sunken battleship *Vasa*. If you have time, pop next door to the **Spritmuseum** (p75; pictured) to get the low-down on the complicated history of booze in Sweden.

Take the ferry from Djurgården across to Norrmalm (or it's an easy walk) and head towards Stureplan, in Östermalm. Have dinner at the seafood-savvy **Sturehof** (p105), before exploring the surrounding clubs, including **Sturecompagniet** (p106) and **Spy Bar** (p106).

Day Three

On day three explore Söder-malm. Start at the brilliant **Fotografiska** (p82). From here, take the stairs up the cliffs to the Söder heights for killer views over the city.

Grab lunch at **Hermans Trädgårdscafé** (p88), then walk back down the steep cobbled streets to Götgatan, Söder-malm's main street, and follow it south to Medborgarplatsen, the neighbourhood's central square. Continue along the main drag, turning left onto Folkungagatan for the pubs and cafes of 'SoFo'.

After dinner at **Chutney** (p89), aim for tree-lined Mariatorget, where you can sit with a drink outside the Rival Hotel, or continue walking north until you reach tiny Monteliusvägen (pictured), a footpath as much as a street, which offers more amazing views over Stockholm.

Day Four

On day four, take a tour of **Stad-shuset** (p114) on the island of Kungsholmen – also a nice neighbourhood to idly wander. Alternatively, if the weather is warm, bring swimwear and soak up the sun on the Stadshuset terrace like the locals.

Next, hop on the tunnelbana to Östermalm for lunch at **Lisa Elmqvist** (p106) inside the fabulous **Östermalms Saluhall** (p105; pictured), where you can browse for speciality foods. Af-ter, school yourself on Viking lore at **Historiska Museet** (p98). Next up is **Svenskt Tenn** (p107) for a lesson in the fundamentals of Swedish interior design.

Treat yourself to dinner at **Ekstedt** (p105) or **Gastrologik** (p105), then boot it back to Norrmalm for cocktails and clubbing at **East** (p59) and **Café Opera** (p58).

Need to Know

For detailed information, see Survival Guide (p139)

Language
Swedish

Currency
Kronor (kr)

Visas
Visitors from Australia, New Zealand, Canada and the US can stay in Sweden without a visa for up to 90 days. Some nationalities need a Schengen visa in advance.

Mobile Phones
Most mobiles work, though often with hefty roaming fees. Local SIM cards work in most phones, with the benefit no roaming charges.

Money
ATMs are widely available. Credit cards are widely accepted.

Time
Central European Time (GMT plus one hour)

Tipping
Tipping is rare and usually reserved for good restaurant service (10–15% is customary). Tipping taxi drivers is optional.

Daily Budget

Budget: Less than 1000kr
Dorm bed or camping site: 250–650kr
Fast-food lunch or sandwich: 65–99kr
24-hour bus and metro ticket: 120kr
Museum admission 100–150kr

Midrange: 1000–2000kr
Double room: 1000–1600kr
Restaurant meal: 185–200kr
Happy-hour drink: 35–95kr

Top End: More than 2000kr
Double room: 1600–2600kr
Upscale dinner and drinks: 350–650kr
Taxi from airport: 500kr

Advance Planning

Three months before Reserve a table at a top restaurant; book big-ticket excursions (Göta Canal); book hostels or cabins in popular places (Stockholm archipelago).

One month before Make reservations for popular activities (kayak tours, walking tours); book tickets to performances (theatre, live music); reserve a rental car.

One week before Reserve seats on trains and long-distance buses.

Arriving in Stockholm

✈ From Stockholm Arlanda Airport

Flights to Stockholm generally land at Arlanda Airport, 45km north of the city. Terminals 2 and 5 are for international flights; 3 and 4 are domestic (there is no Terminal 1). There are car hire desks at the airport.

Arlanda Express (www.arlandaexpress. com; Centralstationen; one-way adult/youth 280/150kr) trains between the airport and Centralstationen run every 10 to 15 minutes from 5am to 12.30am (less frequently after 9pm), taking 20 minutes.

Flygbussarna (www.flygbussarna.se; Cityterminalen) buses run to/from Cityterminalen from stop 11 in Terminal 5 every 10 to 15 minutes (adult/child one way 119/99kr, 40 minutes).

Airport Cab, **Sverige Taxi** (☎020-20 20 20; www.sverigetaxi.se) and **Taxi Stockholm** (☎15 00 00; www.taxistockholm.se) are reliable taxi services.

From Cityterminalen

Local buses go from here into Stockholm's various neighbourhoods; figure 20 minutes to downtown (85kr).

From Centralstationen

Local buses head to Stockholm's neighbourhoods from here; around one hour 20 minutes to downtown (159kr).

Getting Around

Storstockholms Lokaltrafik (SL; ☎08-600 10 00; www.sl.se; Centralstationen; ⏰7am-9pm) runs the city's tunnelbana (metro), trains and buses.

Ⓜ Metro

Stockholm's fast, efficient underground Tunnelbana metro system connects various neighbourhoods.

🚌 Bus

The city bus system, using the same tickets/passes as the tunnelbana, is extensive. You must have your ticket or pass before boarding.

⚙ Cycling/Scootering

A range of bicycle- and scooter-hire services can be found across the city, such as **Tier** (www.tier.app) and **Voi** (www.voiscooters.com).

🚋 Tram

Trams run between Norrmalmstorg and Skansen, passing most attractions on Djurgården.

🚗 Taxi

Taxis are readily available but fees are unregulated – check for a meter or arrange the fare first.

⚓ Ferry

In summer, ferries are the best way to get to Djurgården, and they serve the archipelago year-round.

Stockholm Neighbourhoods

Vasastan (p127)
Find some of the city's best restaurants (not to mention a handful of worthy art galleries and cultural sights) in this no-nonsense neighbourhood.

Kungsholmen (p113)
Stockholm's quieter achieving area. Side streets harbour on-point design stores, former factories house buzzing bars and there are great places to swim.

Norrmalm (p49)
Modernism rules in this restless commercial hub. It's home to major department stores, glam bars and restaurants, and cultural heavyweight the Nationalmuseum.

Södermalm (p81)
Take a pinch of eccentricity, add a splash of laid-back cool and you have this ultra-stylish but casual and fun neighbourhood. Known locally as Söder, this is the city's creative engine room.

Stadshuset

Östermalm (p97)
Dress up and scope out the beautiful people over a flute of bubbly. Östermalm is Stockholm's well-heeled party hotspot.

Djurgården & Skeppsholmen (p63)
Djurgården is a parklike oasis with cultural riches. Skeppsholmen proves that good things come in small packages.

Historiska Museet ◉

Vasamuseet ◉

◉ *Kungliga Slottet*

◉ *Skansen*

◉ *Moderna Museet*

◉ *Fotografiska*

Gamla Stan (p33)
A medieval labyrinth of cobblestone streets, churches, palaces and saffron-hued buildings. The old town is Stockholm's historic and geographic heart.

Explore
Stockholm

Gamla Stan (p33) SCANRAIL1/SHUTTERSTOCK ©

Explore ⚓

Gamla Stan

The old town is Stockholm's historic and geographic heart. Here, cobblestone streets wriggle past Renaissance churches, baroque palaces and medieval squares. Spice-coloured buildings sag like wizened old men, and narrow lanes harbour everything from dusty toy shops to candlelit cafes. Västerlånggatan is the area's nerve centre, a busy thoroughfare lined with galleries, eateries and souvenir shops.

The Short List

○ **Kungliga Slottet (p34)** *The Royal Palace looks a bit grim, but it houses some beautiful examples of Swedish baroque and rococo interiors.*

○ **Nobelmuseet (p42)** *A focus on innovation and creativity defines this sleek museum about the Nobel Prize and its recipients.*

○ **Mårten Trotzigs Gränd (p44)** *The narrow, cobbled streets of Old Town reach their selfie-loving peak in this, the city's tiniest alley.*

○ **Riddarholmskyrkan (p42)** *This starkly beautiful church holds the crypts of old Swedish royalty.*

○ **Riksdagshuset (p43)** *The Swedish Parliament building's tours are illuminating, inspiring and fun.*

Getting There & Around

Ⓜ (Tunnelbana) Gamla Stan, Slussen

🚢 Line 83 to Slussen

🚌 3, 53 to Gamla Stan, Riddarhustorget; 2, 57, 76, 96, 190-195 to Slottsbacken

🚶 The old town is an easy stroll from the city centre

Neighbourhood Map on p40

Top Experience 📷

Tour the royal palace, Kungliga Slottet

Stockholm's imposing 608-room royal palace – the largest in the world still in use – was built on the ruins of Tre Kronor castle, most of which burned to the ground in 1697. The north wing survived and was incorporated into the new building. Designed by the court architect Nicodemus Tessin the Younger, it took 57 years to complete. The royal family has lived here since 1754.

◎ MAP P40, E2

📞 08-402 61 00

www.theroyalpalace.se

Slottsbacken

adult/child 160/80kr

🕑 9am-5pm daily Jul & Aug, from 10am daily May-Jun & Sep, 10am-4pm Tue-Sun Oct-Apr

🚇 Gamla Stan

Changing of the Guard
It's worth timing your visit to see the Changing of the Guard, which takes place in the outer courtyard at 12.15pm Monday to Saturday and 1.15pm on Sundays and public holidays May through August, but only on Wednesday, Saturday, Sunday and public holidays September to May.

Museum Tre Kronor
This museum displays the foundations of 13th-century defensive walls and items rescued from the castle during the 1697 fire. It describes how the fire started (a watchman was off flirting with a kitchen maid) and vividly explains the meaning of 'run the gauntlet' (which in 1697 was the punishment for flirting with kitchen maids while fire destroyed the castle).

Gustav III's State Bedchamber
King Gustav III, whose efforts to reconsolidate power for the throne in the early part of his reign made him unpopular with the nobility, died here in 1792 – a full 13 days after an assassin shot him during a masquerade ball. He survived just long enough to keep up appearances and suppress the attempted coup.

Silver Throne
Queen Kristina's silver throne, in the Hall of State, was rescued from the Tre Kronor fire. It was a gift to the queen from Swedish statesman Magnus Gabriel de la Gardie (son of Ebba Brahe, who had an affair with King Gustavus Adolphus). The impressive hall was designed by architects Nicodemus Tessin the Younger and Carl Hårleman.

Karl XI Gallery
One of the prettiest rooms in the palace, and still used today for royal functions, the decadent Karl XI Gallery was inspired by Versailles' Hall of Mirrors and is considered the finest example of Swedish late baroque.

★ **Top Tips**

o Beat the crowds: for the best experience, arrive right when the palace opens.

o Free 45-minute tours in English are well worth taking – check timetables online for the current schedule.

o Admission to the palace also includes the nearby Museum Tre Kronor, the Royal Treasury and the Antikmuseum.

o Tickets are valid for seven days.

o The apartments are occasionally closed for royal business; closures are noted on the website.

✖ **Take a Break**

From June to late August, a small cafe with outdoor tables in the castle's inner courtyard serves light lunches, coffee and pastries.

The Bernadottes

When King Gustav IV Adolf was forced to abdicate the throne after losing Finland, the Swedish nobles had to find a replacement; there was no heir. So a certain Baron Mörner invited one of Napoleon's marshals, Jean-Baptiste Bernadotte (1763–1844), to take the Swedish throne. He agreed, changing his name to Karl Johan, ruling for 26 years and starting the Bernadotte dynasty that still holds the throne today.

Antikmuseum

Royal Treasury

The Royal Treasury (Skattkammaren) contains ceremonial crowns, sceptres and other regalia of the Swedish monarchy, including Lovisa Ulrika's crown, a 1696 baptismal font (still used today for royal baptisms), tapestries rescued from the 1697 fire and a 16th-century sword that belonged to Gustav Vasa.

Antikmuseum

Gustav III's Museum of Antiquities (summer only) displays sculpture mostly collected by King Gustav III during his Italian journeys (the requisite 'grand tour') during the 1780s. For most of the Swedish public, this was a first glimpse of classical sculpture. The galleries were renovated starting in the 1950s in order to keep the collection safely in its original home.

Royal Chapel

A chapel has stood in the royal palace since the 1200s, but this version of it – dating from the palace reopening in 1754 – was a 50-year project, overseen by Nicodemus Tessin the Younger. (In the early days, though, the royal family took mass in their own private chambers.)

Kungliga Slottet

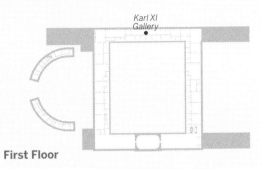

First Floor

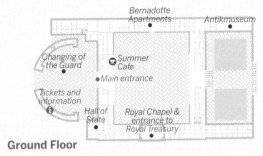

Ground Floor

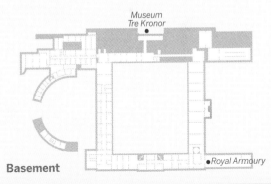

Basement

Walking Tour 🚶

Gamla Stan & Around

Gamla Stan transports you back in time to Stockholm's early history. Most of the tourist activity is concentrated on Västerlånggatan and Stora Nygatan, but if you venture into the back alleys and quieter, more crooked streets, you'll find a city that seems almost unchanged since medieval times.

Walk Facts

Start 🚇 Gamla Stan
End 🚇 Gamla Stan
Length 2.5km; 1½ hours

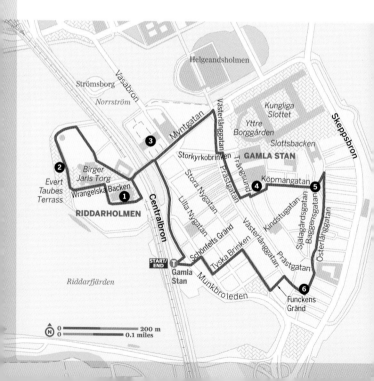

❶ Riddarholmen

Other than its lovely **cathedral** (p42), this undervisited islet doesn't have a lot in the way of tourist activity, but it's extremely pretty to wander around, with its cobblestone streets and compressed huddle of fairy-tale buildings in delicate pastel shades.

❷ Evert Taubes Terrass

At the far west side of Riddarholmen is this flat terrace covered with tiny paving stones and decorated with impressive sculptures at either end. The singing lute player, *Everlife,* portrays the terrace's namesake, Swedish troubadour Evert Taube, in a 1990 bronze by Willy Gordon. The sculpture at the opposite end is *Solbåten* (1966), by Christian Berg.

❸ Riddarhuset

Heading back towards Gamla Stan, you'll pass Riddarhuset, a big pink-and-turquoise building that slightly resembles a wedding cake. This is the House of Nobility (or House of Knights), designed by French father–son architects Simon and Jean de la Vallée and completed in 1660. The statue in front is Axel Oxenstierna (1583–1654), a close adviser to Queen Christina.

❹ Stortorget

Make your way to Mynttorget and turn down Västerlånggatan, the main shopping street, for a few blocks, then zigzag up to quieter Prästgatan. Turn left up the hill to Stortorget, the old town's beautiful main square. It's lined with gorgeous old buildings and usually filled with happy holidaymakers; you'd never know it was once the scene of a massacre (the Stockholm Bloodbath of 1520).

❺ Köpmantorget

Stroll down Köpmangatan ('Merchant's Street') to the triangular 'square' at its end, where you'll find a 1912 bronze replica of Berndt Notke's wooden statue from the 1400s, *St George and the Dragon,* which occupies **Storkyrkan** (p44). Take the road that slopes off to the right, and continue along Österlånggatan, another major commercial thoroughfare.

❻ Järntorget

At the end of Österlånggatan is this pretty square, barely younger than Stortorget (it dates to 1300). It began as an important trade spot, first for corn, then iron. As you continue back towards the starting point, peek up Mårten Trötzigs gränd – the narrowest street in town, which squiggles off to the right from Västerlånggatan.

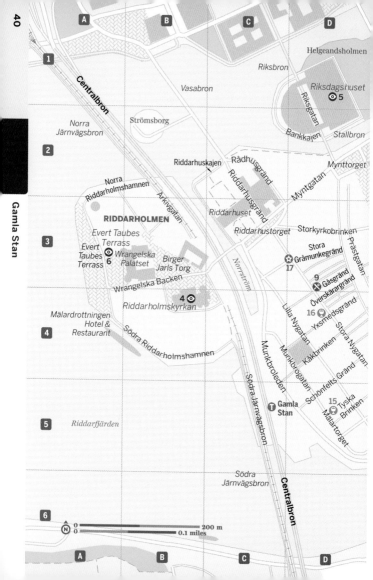

Helgeandsholmen

Riksbron

Riksdagshuset
⊙ 5

Centralbron

Vasabron

Riksgatan

Bankkajen

Stallbron

Norra
Järnvägsbron

Strömsborg

Riddarhuskajen

Rådhusgränd

Mynttorget

Mynttorget

Myntgatan

Norra
Riddarholmshamnen

Arkivgatan

Riddarhusgränd

Riddarhusgränd

RIDDARHOLMEN

Riddarhuset

Evert Taubes
Terrass

Riddarhustorget

Storkyrkobrinken

Evert
Taubes
Terrass ⊙ 6

Wrangelska
Palatset

Birger
Jarls Torg

Stora
Gråmunkegränd
✪ 17

9
Gåsgränd ✪
Överskärargränd

Wrangelska Backen

Norrström

Lilla Nygatan

16 ⊙
Yxsmedsgränd

Stora Nygatan

Prästgatan

Riddarholmskyrkan

4 ⊙

Mälardrottningen
Hotel &
Restaurant

Södra Riddarholmshamnen

Munkbroleden

Munkbrogatan

Kåkbrinken

Schönfelts Gränd

15
Tyska
Brinken

Gamla
Stan 🚇

Mälartorget

Riddarfjärden

Södra
Järnvägsbron

Södra Järnvägsbron

Centralbron

0   200 m
0   0.1 miles
Ⓝ

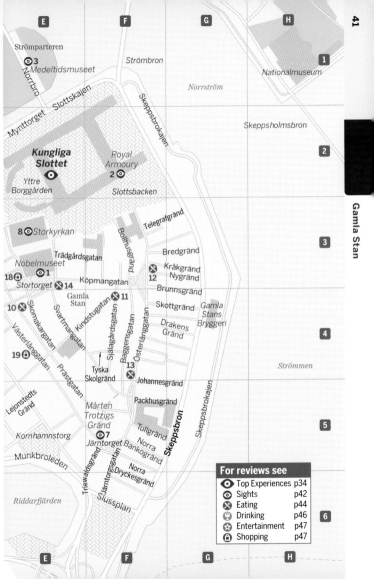

Strömparteren

3 Medeltidsmuseet

Norrbro

Strömbron

Norrström

Nationalmuseum

Skeppsholmsbron

Myntorget

Slottskajen

Skeppsbrokajen

Kungliga Slottet

Royal Armoury
2

Yttre Borggården

Slottsbacken

8 Storkyrkan

Telegrafgränd

Trädgårdsgatan

Bollhusgränd

Bredgränd

Nobelmuseet
1

Kråkgränd
12

Nygränd

18

Köpmangatan

Brunnsgränd

Stortorget 14

Gamla Stan 11

Skottgränd

Gamla Stans Bryggeri

10

Skomakargatan

Svartmangatan

Kindstugatan

Själagårdsgatan

Baggengatan

Österlånggatan

Drakens Gränd

Strömmen

Västerlånggatan

19

Prästgatan

Tyska Skolgränd

13

Johannesgränd

Lejonstedts Gränd

Mårten Trotzigs Gränd
7

Packhusgränd

Kornhamnstorg

Järntorget

Tullgränd

Skeppsbron

Skeppsbrokajen

Munkbroleden

Triewaldsgränd

Järntorgsgatan

Norra Bankogränd

Norra Dryckesgränd

Riddarfjärden

Slussplan

Gamla Stan

E   F   G   H

Sights

Nobelmuseet   MUSEUM

1 ⊙ MAP P40, E3

Nobelmuseet presents the history of the Nobel Prizes and their recipients, with a focus on the intellectual and cultural aspects of invention. It's a polished, contemporary space with fascinating displays, including short films on the theme of creativity, interviews with laureates like Ernest Hemingway and Martin Luther King, and cafe chairs signed by the visiting prize recipients (flip them over to see!). (☏08-53 48 18 00; www.nobelcenter. se; Stortorget; adult/child 120kr/free; ⏱9am-8pm daily Jun-Aug, reduced hours rest of year; 🚇Gamla Stan)

Royal Armoury   MUSEUM

2 ⊙ MAP P40, F2

The Royal Armoury is housed in the cellar vaults of the palace but has separate hours. It's a family attic of sorts, crammed with engrossing memorabilia spanning more than 500 years of royal childhoods, coronations, weddings and murders. Meet Gustav II Adolf's stuffed battle steed, Streiff; see the costume Gustav III wore to the masquerade ball on the night he was shot in 1792; or let the kids try on a suit of armour in the playroom. (Livrustkammaren; ☏08-402 30 30; www.livrustkammaren. se; Slottsbacken 3; admission free; ⏱10am to 6pm daily Jul-Aug, shorter

hours rest of year; 🚇43, 46, 55, 59 Slottsbacken, 🚇Gamla Stan)

Medeltidsmuseet   MUSEUM

3 ⊙ MAP P40, E1

Tucked beneath the bridge that links Gamla Stan and Norrmalm, this child-friendly museum was established when construction workers preparing to build a car park here in the late 1970s unearthed foundations from the 1530s. The ancient walls were preserved as found, and a museum was built around them. The circular plan leads visitors through faithful reconstructions of typical homes, markets and workshops from medieval Stockholm. Tickets are valid for one year. (Medieval Museum; www.medeltidsmuseet.stockholm. se; Strömparteren; admission free; ⏱noon-5pm Tue-Sun, to 8pm Wed; 🚇62, 65, Gustav Adolfs torg)

Riddarholmskyrkan   CHURCH

4 ⊙ MAP P40, B4

The strikingly beautiful Riddarholmskyrkan, on the equally pretty and under-visited islet of Riddarholmen, was built by Franciscan monks in the late 13th century. It has been the royal necropolis since the burial of Magnus Ladulås in 1290, and is home to the armorial glory of the Seraphim knightly order. There's a guided tour in English at noon (included with admission) and occasional concerts. Holiday closures are frequent; check the website for updates. Admission fee is by credit card only. (Riddarholmen Church; ☎08-402 61 30; www.kungahuset.se; Riddarholmen; adult/child 50/25kr; ⏰10am-5pm daily mid-May–mid-Sep, 10am-4pm Sat & Sun Oct-Nov; 🚇3, 53 Riddarhustorget, 🚉Gamla Stan)

Riksdagshuset   NOTABLE BUILDING

5 ◎ MAP P40, D1

Technically situated on Helgeandsholmen, the little island in the middle of Norrström, rather than on Gamla Stan, the Swedish Parliament building is an unexpected pleasure to visit. The building consists of two parts: the older front section (facing downstream) dates from the early 20th century, but the other more-modern part contains the current debating chamber. Tours of the building offer a compelling glimpse into the Swedish system of consensus-building government. (Swedish Parliament; ☎020-34 80 00; www.riksdagen.se; Riksgatan 3; admission free; ⏰1hr tours in English noon, 1, 2 & 3pm Mon-Fri mid-Jun–mid-Aug, 1.30pm Sat & Sun Oct–mid-Jun; 🚇3, 59, Riddarhustorget, 🚉Gamla Stan, T-Centralen)

Evert Taubes Terrass   PARK

6 ◎ MAP P40, A3

Evert Taubes Terrass is a tranquil and relaxed spot and one of the best viewpoints in Stockholm, at eye level with lake Mälaren on the quiet island of Riddarholmen, with open sightlines across the water to Stockholm City Hall, München-bryggeriet and Södermalm's coastline. Sunset is the time to

Riksdagshuset

Timing is Everything

For the best experience of Gamla Stan, plan to arrive either first thing in the morning, when it's less crowded, or right around dusk when the light makes for the loveliest photo ops.

come. Taube, the park's namesake, was a beloved composer and troubadour who grew up on the Gothenburg archipelago; he's immortalised in the joyful statue at the corner of the park. (Riddarholmen; admission free; ⏰24hr; 🚇Gamla Stan)

Mårten Trotzigs Gränd AREA

7 ⊙ MAP P40, F5

This tiny alley in Gamla Stan is Stockholm's narrowest street and a popular spot for a photo op. (🚇Gamla Stan)

Storkyrkan CHURCH

8 ⊙ MAP P40, E3

The one-time venue for royal weddings and coronations, Storkyrkan is both Stockholm's oldest building (consecrated in 1306) and its cathedral. Behind a baroque facade, the Gothic-baroque interior includes extravagant royal-box pews designed by Nicodemus Tessin the Younger, as well as German Berndt Notke's dramatic sculpture *St George and the Dragon,* commissioned by Sten Sture the Elder to

commemorate his victory over the Danes in 1471. Keep an eye out for posters and handbills advertising music performances here. (Great Church; www.stockholmsdomkyrko forsamling.se; Trångsund 1; adult/child 60kr/free; ⏰9am-4pm, to 6pm Jun-Aug; 🚇Gamla Stan)

Eating

Hermitage VEGETARIAN $$

9 MAP P40, D3

While it lacks atmosphere or any culinary punch, casual Hermitage is a good spot for a well-priced, no-fuss meat-free feed. The vegetarian buffet includes both cold and hot dishes, the latter hidden away in the drawers beside the main buffet unit. The price includes salad and homemade bread, and there's a discount for takeaway orders. Vegan fare is also available, including cakes. (📞08-411 95 00; www.hermitage.gastrogate.com; Stora Nygatan 11; buffet weekday lunch/dinner & all day Sat & Sun 140/150kr; ⏰11am-9pm May-Sep, reduced hours rest of year; 📶 📄; 🚇Gamla Stan)

Kryp In SWEDISH $$$

10 MAP P40, E4

Small but perfectly formed, this spot wows diners with creative takes on traditional Swedish dishes. Expect the likes of salmon carpaccio, Kalix roe, reindeer roast or gorgeous, spirit-warming saffron aioli shellfish stew. The service is seamless and the atmosphere classy without being stuffy. The three-course set menu (455kr) is superb. Book ahead. (☏08-20 88 41; www.restaurang krypin.nu; Prästgatan 17; lunch mains 135-168kr, dinner mains 198-290kr; ⌚5-11pm Mon-Fri, noon-4pm & 5-11pm Sat & Sun; 🛜; 🚇Gamla Stan)

Under Kastanjen   SWEDISH $$

11 MAP P40, F4

The real reason to hit Under Kastanjen is for its picturesque setting, on a cobbled square, beside a chestnut tree, surrounded by ochre and yellow storybook houses. While the menu lacks wow factor, it does offer simple, comforting, generous home cooking, from soups and stews to classic Swedish meatballs. There's a good choice of gluten-free dishes, plus cakes for that mid-afternoon sugar hit. (☏08-21 50 04; www.under kastanjen.se; Kindstugatan 1; sandwiches 110-125kr, daily lunch special 105kr, mains 182-289kr; ⌚8am-9pm Mon-Wed, to 11pm Thu & Fri, 9am-11pm Sat, 9am-9pm Sun; 🛜👶; 🚇Gamla Stan)

Fem Små Hus   SWEDISH $$$

12 MAP P40, F3

Fem Små Hus offers the perfect combination of authentic historical setting with traditional cuisine, just a short walk from the Royal Palace in the heart of the old town. The menu features Swedish classics with a French touch – think reindeer fillets with port wine sauce, seared Arctic char, Swedish farm

Kryp In

chicken confit – served in 17th-century vaulted cellars. (☏08-10 87 75; www.femsmahus.se; Nygränd 10; mains 205-410kr; ⌚11.30am-11pm Mon-Tue, to midnight Wed-Fri, 1pm-midnight Sat, 1-11pm Sun; 🚇Gamla Stan)

Magnus Ladulås   SWEDISH $$$

13 MAP P40, F4

Named after King Magnus III, Restaurang Magnus Ladulås is housed on the site of a 16th-century eatery. Tables hug sloped ceilings in this authentic and intimate setting where the menu is built around Swedish classics – think meatballs with potatoes and lingonberries, seafood stew, or pike-perch with roe and lobster sauce. (☏08-21 19 57; http://magnusladulas.se;

Österlånggatan 26; mains 195-289kr; ⏱11am-10pm Mon-Thu, to 11pm Fri, 1-11pm Sat, to 8pm Sun; 🚇Gamla Stan)

Grillska Husets Konditori

BAKERY, CAFE $

14 🍴 MAP P40, E3

The cafe and bakery run by Stockholms Stadsmission, a chain of secondhand charity shops, is an excellent spot for a sweet treat or a traditional shrimp sandwich, especially when warm weather allows for seating at the outdoor tables in Gamla Stan's main square. There's a bakery shop attached, selling goodies and rustic breads to take away. (📞08-68 42 33 64; www. stadsmissionen.se/vad-vi-gor/grillska-huset; Stortorget 3; mains 90-125kr,

lunch special 125kr; ⏱10am-8pm Mon, to 9pm Tue-Sat, 11am-8pm Sun; 🚇Gamla Stan)

Drinking

Gaston

WINE BAR

15 🍷 MAP P40, D5

Intimate, sophisticated yet relaxed, Gaston is where clued-in Stockholmers swill in Gamla Stan. Sommelier Janni Berndt's weakness for hand-harvested wines and smaller winemakers with fascinating backstories translates into an exciting, ever-changing wine list that might include a Suertes del Marqués from Tenerife or a biodynamic Vie on y Est from the Côtes du Rhône. (📞08-20 85 83; www.gastonvin.se; Mälartorget 15; ⏱5-11pm Mon & Sun,

Wooden Horse Museum

SOPHIEOSTY/SHUTTERSTOCK ©

to midnight Tue-Thu, to 1am Fri, 3pm-1am Sat; 🚇Gamla Stan)

Tritonia CRAFT BEER

16 🍺 MAP P40, D4

If a microbrewery releases only a couple of kegs of a rare beer in Sweden, you'll probably find one of them here. A holy grail for beer buffs, Tritonia peddles intriguing craft brews, from fruit beers and tropical New England IPAs, to malty, barrel-aged concoctions from Estonia. If you're feeling overwhelmed, affable barkeep Johan Thor will guide you towards liquid enlightenment. (📞08-10 00 03; www.tritonia.se; Stora Nygatan 20; ⏰6-11pm Tue-Thu, to 1am Fri, 1pm-1am Sat; 🚇Gamla Stan)

Entertainment

Stampen JAZZ

17 ⭐ MAP P40, D3

Stampen is one of Stockholm's music-club stalwarts, swinging to live jazz and blues six nights a week. The free blues jam (currently on Sundays) pulls everyone from local noodlers to the odd music legend. (📞08-20 57 93; www.stampen.se; Stora Nygatan 5; cover free-200kr; ⏰5pm-1am Tue-Fri & Sun, 2pm-1am Sat; 🚇Gamla Stan)

Shopping

Wooden Horse Museum GIFTS & SOUVENIRS

18 🔒 MAP P40, E3

This museum pays tribute to the Swedish Dalarna Horse (Dala Häst), one of Sweden's most iconic national symbols. Boasting hundreds of specimens, ranging from antique pieces to more contemporary designs, the Wooden Horse Museum is the place to pick up an original Stockholm souvenir. (📞08-20 60 89; http://woodenhorsemuseumsweden.se; Stortorget 14; ⏰11am-6pm Tue-Sat; Ⓜ Gamla Stan)

Science Fiction Bookshop BOOKS

19 🔒 MAP P40, E4

In some ways this seems an unlikely location for a science fiction–fantasy comic bookshop, but in other ways it makes perfect sense. Regardless, this is the place to come for comics and graphic novels both mainstream and obscure (in English and Swedish), as well as books, games, toys and posters. Friendly staff will help you hunt down treasures. (www.sfbok.se; Västerlånggatan 48; ⏰10am-7pm Mon-Fri, to 5pm Sat, noon-5pm Sun; 🚇Gamla Stan)

Explore ⊚

Norrmalm

The modern heart of the city, Norrmalm is where most visits to Stockholm begin: it's home to the main train and bus stations, Centralstationen and Cityterminalen, respectively. It's also where you'll find the highest concentration of schmancy retail boutiques, glamorous bars and restaurants, hotels from functional to fabulous, and noteworthy cultural institutions.

The Short List

o *Kulturhuset (p54) The heart of Stockholm's urban core.*

o *Hallwylska Museet (p54) An eye-opener if you think of all Swedish homes as austere and minimalist.*

o *Iris Hantverk (p51) Bathe in handmade local craft heaven.*

o *Fasching (p59) The best club in the city for jazz and the jazz-adjacent.*

o *Nationalmuseum (p54) A fantastic collection of fine art and design objects.*

Getting There

Ⓜ (Tunnelbana) T-Centralen, Kungsträdgården

🚌 54, 57, 65, 69, 75 to Cityterminalen, Norrmalmstorg, Sergels Torg

🚊 7

Neighbourhood Map on p52

Sergels Torg (p55) B-HIDE THE SCENE/SHUTTERSTOCK ©

Walking Tour 🥾

Norrmalm Shop Hopping

Ever wondered how Stockholmers manage to look so fashionable all the time? Shopping is a sport here, and Norrmalm is one of the best places to do it well. Its chic storefronts peddle everything from traditional handmade crafts to fine crystal, outdoors equipment to the most exclusive high-fashion brands. And a good stretch of the district is pedestrian-only, so you can focus on the task at hand.

Walk Facts

Start Norrmalmstorg,
🚇 Östermalmstorg,
🚊 7 to Kungsträdgården

End Kungsgatan,
🚇 T-Centralen, Hötorget

Length 2.5km; one hour

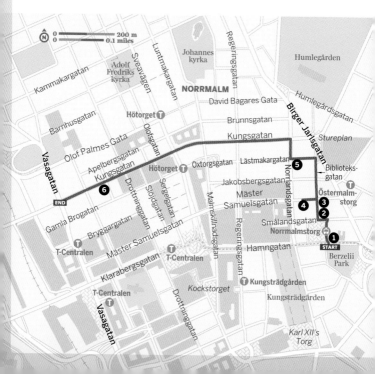

❶ Norrmalmstorg

Start your mission at the heart of the district, the wide-open square of Norrmalmstorg. At its eastern-most edge you'll find the epitome of Stockholm cool, **Acne** (www. acnestudios.com; Norrmalmstorg 2; ⏱10am-7pm Mon-Fri, to 5pm Sat, noon-4pm Sun), with a shop that closely resembles a fashion museum. In the same block you'll find the impossible-to-resist **Marimekko** (www.marimekko.com; Norrmalmstorg 4; ⏱10am-7pm Mon-Fri, to 5pm Sat). This Finnish textile company plasters almost everything with its iconic prints.

❷ Biblioteksgatan

At the north end of Norrmalmstorg is this pedestrianised shopping street, lined wall-to-wall with hot brand names. Right on the corner is an outlet of the groundbreaking Swedish fashion designer **Filippa K** (www.filippa-k.com; Biblioteksgatan 2; ⏱10am-7pm Mon-Sat, noon-5pm Sun).

❸ Mäster Samuelsgatan

This street, which crosses Bibli-oteksgatan, is home to a dense population of big-name fashion. Off to the right is **Whyred** (www.whyred. se; Mäster Samuelsgatan 3; ⏱10am-7pm Mon-Fri, to 5pm Sat, noon-4pm Sun), beloved for men's sweaters and women's shoes, among other things; next to that is the relatively new **BLK DNM** (www.blkdnm.com; Mäster Samuelsgatan 1), with its painfully hip jackets and clothing by designer Johan Lindeberg.

❹ Cow Parfymeri

A great place to pick up gifts to bring home, **Cow Parfymeri** (www. cowparfymeri.se; Mäster Samuelsgatan 9; ⏱11am-6pm Mon-Fri, to 4pm Sat) is a cool cosmetics temple with a trendsetting range of perfumes, sticks and shades. Pick up rock-chic cosmetics, or spray yourself silly with hard-to-find fragrances from Paris and New York.

❺ Espresso Stop

By now you're probably ready for a break. The lovely **Bianchi Cafe & Cycles** (www.bianchicafecycles.com; Norrlandsgatan 16; ⏱11am-10pm Mon-Sat) is an ideal spot for an espresso and a pastry.

❻ Kungsgatan

You'll pass by all manner of retail out-lets here, both local and global, in-cluding the fun outdoor market and food hall at Hötorget. Several blocks along, stop in at **Iris Hantverk** (Kungsgatan 55; ⏱10am-8pm Mon-Fri, to 3pm Sat) for gorgeous handmade Swedish crafts: expect impeccably made woodwork, linens, textiles, candlesticks, soaps, glassware and crafting books. Across the street is **WESC** (www.wesc.com; Kungsgatan 66; ⏱11am-6pm Mon-Fri, 10am-4pm Sat), another museumlike store carrying skateboard-inspired fashion. This street-smart label got started by dressing up underground artists and muses. It has since become one of Swedish fashion's big guns, opening up stores from Seoul to Beverly Hills.

A **B** **C** **D**

1

Rådmansgatan

Tegnérgatan

Tegnérlunden

Johannes
kyrka

Tegnérgatan

Adolf
Fredriks
kyrka

Kammakargatan

Luntmakargatan

Döbelnsgatan

Malmskillnadsgatan

Drottninggatan

Sveavägen

Olofsgatan

Hollándergatan

2

Västmannagatan

Wallingatan

20

Barnhusgatan

T Hötorget

Brunnsgatan

19

Norra
Bantorget

Norra
Bantorget

Olof Palmes Gata

Apelbergsgatan

21

Hötorget

Oxtorget

T Hötorget

3

Vasagatan

Östra Järnvägsgatan

16

Kungsgatan

Klara Norra Kyrkogatan

Gamla Brogatan

Bryggargatan

Sergelgatan

Sveavägen

Sköldgatan

Klaratunnelen

Terminalslingan

Vasaplan

T-Centralen
T

Máster Samuelsgatan

T-Centralen
23

T

Sergels
Torg
6

Malmskillnadsgatan

4

Klarabergsgatan

Klara
Kyrka

3
18

Kulturhuset

Brunkebergstorg

26

Klarabergsviadukten

Centralplan

T-Centralen

Drottninggatan

Vattugatan

Herkulesgatan

Malmtorgsgatan

5

Stockholm
Centralstationen

Vasagatan

Sheraton
Hotel

Medelhavsmuseet

Jakobsgatan

4

Centralbron

Tegelbacken

Fredsgatan

Klara Sjö

Hantverkargatan

Strömgatan

6

Norra
Järnvägsbron

Centralbron

Vasabron

A **B** **C** **D**

Norrmalm

For reviews see

◉	Sights	p54
✖	Eating	p55
◗	Drinking	p58
★	Entertainment	p59
🅐	Shopping	p60

200 m
0.1 miles

Birger Jarlsgatan

Engelbrektsgatan

Humlegården

Kungliga Biblioteket

Engelbrektsplan

David Bagares Gata

Sturegatan

Brahegatan

Grev Turegatan

Humlegårdsgatan

Kungsgatan

Norrlandsgatan

Sturegatan

Stureplan

ÖSTERMALM

14 🚇
Biblioteksgatan
15

Lästmakargatan

Regeringsgatan

Jakobsbergsgatan

Mäster Samuelsgatan

25 🅐

10 ✖

Birger Jarlsgatan

🚇 Östermalmstorg

Östermalmstorg

🚇 Östermalmstorg

Nybrogatan

Sibyllegatan

Hedvig Eleonora kyrka

Storgatan

Armémuseum

Kungliga Hovstallet

Skeppargatan

Artillerigatan

Riddargatan

Kaptensgatan

Greygatan

Smålandsgatan

Hallwylska Museet

Dramatiska teatern

Norrmalmstorg 🚇

🅐 22   24 🅐 Norrmalmstorg ◉ 5

Hamngatan

Berzelii Park Raoul Wallenbergs Torg

Nybroplan ◗

Näckströmsgatan

12 ◗

Wetterling Gallery

Wahrendorffsgatan

Kungsträdgården

🚇
9 ★
Kocksgränd

Västra Trädgårdsgatan

Regeringsgatan

Kungsträdgården ◉ 2

Kungsträdgården

Kungsträdgården 🚇

Nybroviken

Strandvägen
Tram Line 7

Strandvägen

Ladugårdslandsviken

Djurgårdsfärjan Ferry (Summer Only)

Jakobs Kyrka

Fredsgatan

17

11 ★ Karl XII's Torg

13 ✖

Gustav Adolfs Torg

Strömgatan

Norrbro

Norrström

Strömparteren

Strömbron

Riksdagshuset

Blasieholmsgatan

Stallgatan

8 7
södra Blasieholmshamnen

Grand Hôtel Stockholm

Nybrokajen

Hovslagaregatan

Museiparken

Nationalmuseum ◉ 1

Museikajen

Skeppsholmsbron

Sights

Nationalmuseum
MUSEUM

1 ⊙ MAP P52, G6

Sweden's largest art museum is home to the nation's collection of painting, sculpture, drawings, decorative arts and graphics from the Middle Ages to the present. (National Art Museum; www.national museum.se; Södra Blasieholmshamnen; 🚌65)

Wetterling Gallery
GALLERY

2 ⊙ MAP P52, E4

This cool gallery space at the edge of Kungsträdgården always has something interesting going on – usually a boundary-pushing contemporary painter, but there's also often photography or multimedia work, from big names (eg Frank Stella) to soon-to-be-big names. (📞08-10 10 09; www.wetterling gallery.com; Kungsträdgården 3; ⏰11am-5pm Wed-Fri, 1-4pm Sat; 🚇Kungsträdgården)

Kulturhuset
ARTS CENTRE

3 ⊙ MAP P52, D4

This architecturally divisive building, opened in 1974, is an arts hub, with a couple of galleries and workshops, a cinema, three restaurants, and libraries containing international periodicals, newspapers, books and an unusually good selection of graphic novels in many languages. It's home to Stadsteatern (the City Theatre), with performances in various-sized venues (mostly in Swedish). (📞tickets noon-5pm 08-50 62 02 00; www.kulturhusetstadsteatern.se; Sergels Torg; ⏰11am-5pm, some sections closed Mon; 🚻; 🚌52, 56, 59, 69, 91 Sergels Torg, 🚊7 Sergels Torg, 🚇T-Centralen)

Medelhavsmuseet
MUSEUM

4 ⊙ MAP P52, D5

Housed in an elegant Italianate building, Medelhavsmuseet lures history buffs with its Egyptian, Greek, Cypriot, Roman and Etruscan treasures. A large portion of the main hall is devoted to the Swedish expedition to Cyprus in 1927, which unearthed masses of well-preserved artefacts that are attractively displayed here. Don't miss the gleaming gold room, home to a 4th-century BCE olive wreath made of gold. And in the basement: mummies! The attached Bagdad Cafe (open 11.30am to 1.30pm) has great food and atmosphere. (Museum of Mediterranean Antiquities; 📞010-456 12 98; www.medelhavsmuseet. se; Fredsgatan 2; admission free; ⏰noon-8pm Tue-Fri, to 5pm Sat & Sun; 🚇T-Centralen, Kungsträdgården)

Hallwylska Museet
MUSEUM

5 ⊙ MAP P52, F4

A private palace completed in 1898, Hallwylska Museet was once home to compulsive hoarder Wilhelmina von Hallwyl, who collected items as diverse as kitchen utensils, Chinese pottery,

JONATHAN SMITH/LONELY PLANET ©

Nationalmuseum

17th-century paintings, silverware, sculpture and her children's teeth. In 1920 she and her husband donated the mansion and its contents to the state. Guided tours in English take place at 12.30pm Tuesday to Sunday, June to August (weekends only the rest of the year). The museum is not wheelchair accessible. (Hallwyl Collection; ☑08-402 30 99; www. hallwylskamuseet.se; Hamngatan 4; tours 40kr; ☺10am-7pm Tue-Sun Jul-Aug, to 4pm rest of year; ℞Östermalmstorg)

Sergels Torg   SQUARE

6 ◉ MAP P52, D4

Stockholm's living room, this circular square (which was undergoing major repairs on our last visit, but was still accessible to foot traffic) is a little on the grungy side, and you'll want to keep close tabs on your wallet, but it's a key transit hub as well as a great place to catch the pulse of the city. Something's always going on here, be it an impromptu classical music performance or a hundreds-strong political demonstration.

Eating

Rutabaga   VEGETARIAN $$$

7 ⊗ MAP P52, F5

At Rutabaga, celebrity chef Mathias Dahlgren pushes vegetarian cuisine into the realm of art: the menu features vividly colourful salads and other unusual combinations (an egg-truffle-white-bean dish, a mango and mozzarella salad) which, as always, Dahlgren

Understand Swedish Design

You don't have to spend much time window-shopping in this city to realise that Stockholm is a living museum of contemporary design. There are zero unstyled objects – no ordinary anything. From milk cartons by Tom Hedqvist to ballerina 'tutu' lamps by Jonas Bohlin and cute IKEA kitchen hooks, the everyday things you see around you here are object lessons in style and innovation. At the core of Swedish design – and architecture – is simple structural elegance above all. The characteristically Swedish interests of nature and craft also inform contemporary design.

Democracy in a Flat-Pack

Seeking to bring simple, good design to the whole world, in an affordable way, Swedish company IKEA has had enormous influence, across Scandinavia and beyond. Ingvar Kamprad started the company in 1943 when he was 17 years old, creating cheap and innovative products born out of Swedish modern design – with the idea of the house as the starting point of good design, rather than the end. Today, the unmistakably huge blue-and-yellow IKEA stores have sprouted up in more than 50 countries all over the world, with new openings always on the agenda. Because of this, Swedish design may have lost some of its exotic appeal. But that just means more people can know the sleek, utilitarian joy of invisible drawers, paper chandeliers and round squares.

Where to Find It

There are many ways to immerse yourself in Swedish design and gain an appreciation for its history: one is simply to walk around the city with your eyes open. But it's also worthwhile to spend some time windowshopping, especially at landmark shops like Svenskt Tenn (p107) and Nordiska Galleriet (p107).

Department stores like NK (p60) are also great sources of the things everyday Swedes furnish their homes with. For something more akin to a history lesson, visit Nordiska Museet (p75) and its displays of design objects from throughout Swedish history. Or make a pilgrimage to some of the sleeker hotels, bars and restaurants in town – Sturehof (p105) was gussied up by Jonas Bohlin; Thomas Sandell did Café Opera (p58); and you can enjoy a smörgåsbord of interior designers at design-focused boutique hotels like the **Birger Jarl Hotel** (📞08-674 18 00; www.birgerjarl.se; Tulegatan 8; cabin r from 1190kr, s/d from 1200/1400kr; 🅿 ⊜ ❄ @ 🛜; 🚋43 Tegnérgatan, 🚉Rådmansgatan).

presents impeccably on the plate. Most dishes are meant for sharing (if you can bear to give any up). Closes in July. (📞08-679 35 84; www.mdghs.se; Södra Blasieholms-hamnen 6, Grand Hôtel Stockholm; dishes 125-295kr; ⏰5pm-midnight Mon-Sat Aug-Jun; 🍴; 🚇Kung-strädgården)

Grands Verandan   SWEDISH $$$

8 MAP P52, F5

Head here, inside the Grand Hôtel, for the famous smörgåsbord – especially during the Christmas holidays, when it becomes even more elaborate (reservations recommended). Arrive early for a window seat and tuck into both hot and cold Swedish staples, including gravadlax with almond potatoes, herring, meatballs and lingonberry jam. It's like a belt-busting crash course in classic Nordic flavours. (📞08-679 35 86; www.grandhotel.se; Södra Blasieholmshamnen 6, Grand Hôtel Stockholm; smörgåsbord 545kr; mains 205-365kr; ⏰7-10.30am & 11.30am-11pm; 🚇Kungsträdgården)

Holy Greens   VEGETARIAN $

9 MAP P52, E4

This crisp, friendly cafe serves huge, healthful bowls of greens, grains and superfoods at good prices – try the Laxokado, with baked salmon, black rice, avocado, pickled vegies, sunflower seeds and greens, or the falafel bowl with a creamy lemon sauce, baby tomatoes and snap peas.

Everything is available gluten-free. Add a shot of grapefruit-beet juice (20kr) for extra virtue. (📞08-22 62 22; www.regeringsgatan.holygreens. se; Regeringsgatan 28; mains 85-105kr; ⏰8am-7pm Mon-Fri, 11am-5pm Sat & Sun; 🍴; 🚇T-Centralen)

Wiener Caféet   CAFE $$

10 MAP P52, F3

Step into the lavish art-deco interior here and you are transported to the grand cafes of Vienna and Paris. Pastry chef Per Bäckström has ensured that this is the place to come in town for tea (2pm-5pm). And not just a cuppa, but a lavish Ritz Hotel-style experience including scones and cream, choux puffs and assorted cakes. (📞08-68 42 38 50; www.wienercafeet. com; Biblioteksgatan 6-8; mains 185-269kr, sandwiches 85-95kr, afternoon tea 329kr; ⏰7am-9pm Mon-Fri, 9.30am-9pm Sat, 9.30am-7pm Sun; 📶; 🚇291, 🚇Östermalmstorg)

Operakällaren   FRENCH, SWEDISH $$$

11 MAP P52, E5

Inside Stockholm's show-off opera house, the century-old Operakällaren is a major gastronomic event. Decadent chandeliers, golden mirrors and exquisitely carved ceilings set the scene for French-meets-fusion adventures like seared scallops with caramel, cauliflower purée, *pata negra* ham and brown-butter emulsion. Book at least two weeks ahead. (📞08-676 58 00; www.operakallaren.se; Karl XII's Torg

10, Opera House; tasting menus 1050-5950kr; ☺6pm-1am Tue-Sat, closed mid-Jul–mid-Aug; 🚇Kungsträdgården)

Drinking

Berns Salonger BAR

12 🚇 MAP P52, F4

A Stockholm institution since 1862, this glitzy entertainment palace remains one of the city's hottest party spots. While the gorgeous ballroom hosts some brilliant live-music gigs, the best of Berns' bars is in the intimate basement, packed with cool creative types, top-notch DJs and projected art-house images. Check the website for a schedule of events; some require advance ticket purchase. (📞08-56 63 22 00; www.berns.se;

Berzelii Park; ☺club 11pm-4am Thu-Sat, occasionally Wed & Sun, bar from 5pm daily; 🚇Kungsträdgården)

Café Opera CLUB

13 🚇 MAP P52, E5

Rock stars need a suitably excessive place to schmooze, booze and groove, one with glittering chandeliers, ceiling frescoes and a jet-set vibe. This bar-club combo fits the bill, but it's also welcoming enough to make regular folk *feel* like rock stars. If you only have time to hit one primo club during your visit, this is a good choice. (📞08-676 58 07; www.cafeopera.se; Karl XII's Torg; cover from 160kr; ☺10pm-3am Wed-Sun; 🚇Kungsträdgården)

Konserthuset (p60)

East

BAR

14 MAP P52, F3

East is a bar, restaurant and club rolled into one. Great cocktails make it a bartender hang-out. Dishes have a predominantly modern Asian twist (locals recommend the sushi), carrying influences from Vietnam, Korea and Japan. Set right in the heart of Östermalm on Stureplan, it's a good place for fuelling up before or during a club night. (08-611 49 59; http://east.se; Stureplan 13; dinner mains 247-385kr; 11.30am-3am Mon-Sat, 5pm-3am Sun; Östermalmstorg)

Solidaritet

CLUB

15 MAP P52, F3

Solidaritet plays host to both Swedish and internationally renowned DJs with an emphasis on electronic music. The interior decor, designed by leading Swedish architects, is sleek and stylish. The club is set just off Stureplan, the centre of Stockholm's club and party scene. (08-678 10 50; www.solidaritet.eu; Lästmakargatan 3; 11pm-5am Wed-Sat; Östermalmstorg)

Entertainment

Fasching

JAZZ

16 MAP P52, B3

Music club Fasching is the pick of Stockholm's jazz clubs, with live music most nights. DJs often take over with Afrobeat, Latin, neo-soul or R&B on Friday night and

Advance Tickets

Buy tickets in advance for acts you don't want to miss at Fasching or Glenn Miller Café. Same goes for opera, dance and theatre performances around Norrmalm – they do sell out.

retro-soul, disco and rare grooves on Saturday. (08-53 48 29 60; www.fasching.se; Kungsgatan 63; 6pm-1am Mon-Thu, to 4am Fri & Sat, 5pm-1am Sun; T-Centralen)

Operan

OPERA

17 MAP P52, E5

The Royal Opera is the place to go for thunderous tenors, sparkling sopranos and classical ballet. It has some bargain tickets in seats with poor views, and occasional lunchtime concerts for 275kr (including light lunch). (08-791 44 00; www.operan.se; Gustav Adolfs Torg, Operahuset; tickets 240-1070kr; Kungsträdgården)

Stockholms Stadsteatern

THEATRE

18 MAP P52, D4

Regular performances are staged at this theatre inside Kulturhuset, as well as guest appearances by foreign theatre companies. It's also the temporary home to some of the collections from the National Gallery, which is closed

Style City

Stockholm is a ludicrously fashionable city. Casual dress is OK for daytime, but you'll be conspicuous at nightclubs or top-end restaurants if you don't snazz it up. From September to May, bring a hat, gloves and scarf for nights out. Many clubs enforce a coat-check in winter; be prepared to hand over your top layer.

for renovations. (📞08-50 62 02 00; www.stadsteatern.stockholm.se; Kulturhuset, Sergels Torg; tickets 200-350kr; 🚇T-Centralen)

Glenn Miller Café   JAZZ, BLUES

19 ⭐ MAP P52, D2

Simply loaded with character, this tiny jazz-and-blues bar draws a faithful, fun-loving crowd. It also serves excellent, affordable French-style classics like mussels with white wine sauce. Live music Wednesday to Saturday. (📞08-10 03 22; Brunnsgatan 21A; ⏱5pm-1am Mon-Thu, to 2am Fri & Sat; 🚇Hötorget)

Dansens Hus   DANCE

20 ⭐ MAP P52, B2

This place is an absolute must for contemporary-dance fans. Guest artists have included everyone from British choreographer Akram Khan to Canadian innovator Daniel Léveillé. (📞08-50 89 90 90; www.

dansenshus.se; Barnhusgatan 12-14; tickets around 300kr, under 20yr half-price; 🚇T-Centralen)

Konserthuset   CLASSICAL MUSIC

21 ⭐ MAP P52, C3

Head to this pretty blue building for classical concerts and other musical marvels, including the Royal Philharmonic Orchestra. The bronze sculpture of nymphs frolicking out front (*Orpheus Well*) is by Carl Milles. (📞08-50 66 77 88; www.konserthuset.se; Hötorget; tickets 85-325kr; 🚇Hötorget)

Shopping

NK   DEPARTMENT STORE

22 🔒 MAP P52, E4

An ultraclassy department store founded in 1902, NK (Nordiska Kompaniet) is a city landmark – you can see its rotating neon sign from most parts of Stockholm. You'll find top-name brands and several nice cafes, and the basement levels are great for stocking up on souvenirs and gourmet groceries. Around Christmas, check out its inventive window displays. (📞08-762 80 00; www. nk.se; Hamngatan 12-18; ⏱10am-8pm Mon-Fri, 10am-6pm Sat, 11am-5pm Sun; 🚇T-Centralen)

Åhléns   DEPARTMENT STORE

23 🔒 MAP P52, C4

For your all-in-one retail therapy, scour department-store giant Åhléns. It's especially good for housewares, bedding and Swedish-made items to bring home as gifts. (📞08-676 60 00; Klarabergsgatan 50; 🕐10am-9pm Mon-Fri, 10am-7pm Sat, 11am-7pm Sun; 🚇T-Centralen)

PK Huset   SHOPPING CENTRE

24 🔒 MAP P52, E4

One of the main shopping centres in Stockholm's central shopping district. Home to Swedish fashion brands and Swedish staples such as Systembolaget and Apotek. Next door to NK department store. (📞0768-71 50 10; www.pkhuset.com; cnr Hamngatan & Norrlandsgatan; 🕐10am-8pm Mon-Fri, to 6pm Sat, to 5pm Sun; 🚇T-Centralen)

Mood Stockholm   MALL

25 🔒 MAP P52, E3

Not quite shopping mall, not quite galleria, Mood Stockholm oozes cool. Straddling the shopping districts of Östermalm and Nor-

rmalm, it's centrally located and a perfect escape from the busy streets – ideal for a shop, drink or meal with friends. Home to both Swedish and internationally renowned brands. (📞08-696 31 00; http://moodstockholm.se; Regeringsgatan 48; 🕐10am-8pm Mon-Fri, to 6pm Sat, 11am-5pm Sun; 🚇Hötorget, Östermalmstorg)

Gallerian   MALL

26 🔒 MAP P52, D4

Stockholm's first shopping mall, Gallerian is right in the middle of the city's shopping districts. It hosts some of Sweden's best-known brands as well as international favourites. A great opportunity to update your wardrobe with some Swedish style or a central point to take a break. (📞08-53 33 73 00; Hamngatan 37; 🕐10am-8pm Mon-Fri, to 6pm Sat, 11am to 6pm Sun; 🚇T-Centralen)

Explore

Djurgården & Skeppsholmen

The parklike island of Djurgården is a museum-goer's dream. Not only are many of Stockholm's top museums gathered here but the setting is sublime: gardens, greenery, a lazy river, cycle paths, picnic places, and all of it just one footbridge (or short summer ferry ride) away from the centre of town. Skeppsholmen is home to a couple of major museums. To get here, take the footbridge from the city centre or hop on the Djurgården ferry from Slussen.

The Short List

○ **Junibacken (p76)** Spend some time in Pippi Longstocking's world.

○ **Moderna Museet (p70)** Visit world-renowned works of art in a sleek modern building.

○ **Prins Eugens Waldemarsudde (p77)** Admire Scandinavian artwork at the prince's garden estate.

○ **Skansen (p64)** Tour a condensed version of traditional Sweden.

○ **Vasamuseet (p68)** A sunken battleship is the city's most impressive museum.

Getting There

🚌 67, 68, 69

🚊 7 from Norrmalmstorg

⛴ Djurgårdsfärjan Ferry services connect Djurgården to Slussen and Skeppsholmen every 10 minutes; SL passes are valid

Ⓜ (Tunnelbana) Kungsträdgården, T-Centralen

Neighbourhood Map on p74

Nordiska Museet (p75) VIACHESLAV SAVITSKIY/SHUTTERSTOCK ©

Top Experience 📷

Explore in the open air at Skansen

The world's first open-air museum, Skansen is a highlight of the city, one of a few attractions most locals will recommend. It occupies a large parklike area on a hillside, and traces the history of Swedish life through various traditional buildings, huts and houses. There's also a zoo of native animals, and a number of places to stop for refreshments.

◎ MAP P74, D3

www.skansen.se

Djurgårdsvägen

adult/child 195/60kr

🕙10am-10pm daily late Jun-Aug, reduced hours rest of year

🅿 🚻

🚌69, ⛴Djurgårdsfärjan, 🚋7

Nordic Zoo

The Skansen Zoo, with moose, reindeer, wolverines, lynx and other native wildlife, is a highlight, especially in spring when baby critters scamper around – the brown bear cubs are irresistible. Around 75 species of Scandinavian animals live in the zoo, along with a few imported species. There's also a petting zoo where young children can meet small animals.

Glassblowers' Workshop

The glassblowers' workshop is a popular stop: watching the intricate forms emerge from glowing blobs of liquid glass is transfixing. The shop was moved here from a Slussen basement in 1936 – the craftswoman in charge today is the third generation of the original family. If you're wondering, the temperature of the oven is 1130°C (2066°F).

Rescued Buildings

Within Skansen, there's a still-working bakery, a bank and post office, a machine shop, botanical gardens and Hazelius' mansion. Part of the pharmacy was moved here from Drottningholm castle; two little garden huts came from Tantolunden, a community garden still operating in Södermalm. There's also a Sami camp, farmsteads representing several regions, a manor house and a school.

Music & Events

Daily activities take place on Skansen's stages, including folk dancing and an enormous public festival at Midsummer's Eve (first Friday after 19 June). If you're in Stockholm for any of the country's major celebrations, such as Walpurgis Night (30 April) or St Lucia Day (13 December), it's a popular place to watch Swedes celebrate. In summer, check out Allsång, a televised sing-along on Skansen's main stage.

★ **Top Tips**

- Prices and hours vary seasonally and closing times for each workshop can vary, so check times online to avoid disappointment.

- From mid-June through August, Waxholmsbolaget ferries (www.waxholmsbolaget.se) run from Slussen to Djurgården; the route is part of the regular SL transit system, so you can use your SL pass to board. It's about a five-minute trip and runs every 10 minutes or so.

- A map and an excellent booklet in English are available to guide you.

- You can take the escalator to the top of the park and make your way downhill.

✕ **Take a Break**

Skansen has a number of cafes, restaurants, hot-dog and ice-cream stands on-site. Stop in at the traditional bakery for a coffee and pastry or lunch.

Living History

Buildings in the open-air museum represent various trades and areas of industry from Sweden's earliest days. In most of them you'll find staff dressed up in period costume, often making crafts, playing music or churning butter while cheerfully answering questions about the folk whose lives they're recreating. It's potentially a bit silly, but endearing in this setting.

Snake at Skansen Aquarium

FILIP RYBORZ/SHUTTERSTOCK ©

Aquarium

The **Skansen Aquarium** (☏08-666 10 00; www.skansen-akvariet.com; adult/child 120/60kr; ☺10am-7pm daily late Jun–mid-Aug, reduced hours rest of year; 🚌7) is worth a wander, with residents such as piranhas, lemurs and pygmy marmosets (the smallest monkeys in the world). Intrepid visitors may be allowed into the cages of some of the animals – check the daily schedule posted at Skansen's main gate. (Unlike most museums inside Skansen, the aquarium has a separate admission fee; adult/child 100/60kr.)

Vastveit Storehouse

There's a top-heavy little wooden hut at the far northern side of Skansen – called Vastveit, it's a storehouse that was imported from Norway, and is reportedly the oldest building in the park, with parts dating from the 14th century. The shape is typical of traditional Swedish mountain and farmstead huts; many are still in use.

Dalahäst

Look for the giant wooden horse, or Dalahäst, a favourite photo op for smaller kids. You'll find it and other playground equipment on Orsakullen, an open area right in the centre of Skansen, which is also conveniently near some restrooms and snack kiosks. Souvenir wooden horses in more portable sizes can be found in the main Skansen gift shop (and all over town).

400 m
0.2 miles

DJURGÅRDEN

Valmundsvägen

Prins Eugens

Bellmans Väg

Bellmansro

Rosendalsterrassen

Orangerivägen

Djurgården

De Besches Väg

Singelbacken

Sirishovsvägen

Rosendalsvägen

Skansen
Zoo

Solidsbacken

Djurgårdsvägen

Djurgårdsbrunnsviken

Tobaks &
Tändsticksmuseum

Skansen
Aquarium

Sollidsbacken

Skansen

Djurgårdsslätten

Hazeliusbacken

Djurgårdsvägen

Hazelius porten

Djurgårdsvägen

Långa Gatan

Sjömansgränd

Bergsgränd

Biologiska
museet

Nobelgatan

Nobelparken

Nordiska Museet/
Vasamuseet

Djurgårdsvägen

Galärvarvsvägen

Liljevalchs/
Gröna Lund

Glassblowers
Workshop

Galärparken

Galärkyrkogården

Strandvägen

Djurgårdsbron

Ladugårdslandsviken

Saltsjön

Skeppsholmen

Svensksundsparken

Kastellholmen

Kastellparken

Örlogsvägen

Top Experience 📷
Study a shipwreck at Vasamuseet

A good-humoured glorification of some dodgy calculations, Vasamuseet is the home of the massive warship Vasa. The ship was the pride of the Swedish crown when it set off on its maiden voyage on 10 August 1628. Within minutes, the top-heavy vessel tipped and sank to the bottom of Saltsjön, along with many of the people on board. The museum details its retrieval and restoration.

◎ MAP P74, B2

📞 08-51 95 48 80

www.vasamuseet.se

Galärvarvsvägen 14

adult/child 130kr/free

🕙 8.30am-6pm daily Jun-Aug, 10am-5pm Thu-Tue, to 8pm Wed Sep-May

🅿

🚢 Djurgårdsfärjan, 🚊7

Exhibits

Five levels of exhibits cover artefacts salvaged from the *Vasa*, life on board, naval warfare and 17th-century sailing and navigation, plus sculptures and temporary exhibitions. The bottom-floor exhibition is particularly fascinating, using modern forensic science to re-create the faces and life stories of several of the ill-fated passengers. The ship was painstakingly raised in 1961 and reassembled like a giant 14,000-piece jigsaw. Almost all of what you see today is original.

Meanwhile

Putting the catastrophic fate of the *Vasa* in historical context is a permanent multimedia exhibit, *Meanwhile*. With images of events and moments happening simultaneously around the globe – from China to France to 'New Amsterdam', from traders and settlers to royal families to working mothers and put-upon merchants – it establishes a vivid setting for the story at hand.

Scale Model

On the entrance level is a model of the ship (pictured left) at scale 1:10, painted according to a thoroughly researched understanding of how the original would've looked. Once you've studied it, look for the intricately carved decorations adorning the actual *Vasa*. The stern in particular is gorgeous – it was badly damaged but has been slowly and carefully restored.

Upper Deck

A reconstruction of the upper gun deck allows visitors to get a feel for what it might have been like to be on a vessel this size. The *Vasa* had two gun decks, which held an atypically large number of cannons – thought to be part of the reason it capsized.

★ **Top Tips**

○ Guided tours in English depart from the front entrance every 30 minutes in summer.

○ Near the entrance of the museum is a cinema screening a 25-minute film covering topics not included in the exhibitions.

○ You can climb aboard the reconstructed upper gun deck, but the actual ship is off-limits for its safety.

✕ **Take a Break**

There's a restaurant inside the museum, serving coffee, drinks and full meals. Outside the museum, you're not far from Wärdshuset Ulla Winbladh (p79), which also has inviting outdoor seating areas.

Top Experience
Admire modern art at Moderna Museet

Stockholm's modern-art maverick, with a fabulous permanent collection of paintings, sculpture, photography, video art and installations. See works by famous folks, as well as their Scandinavian contemporaries and plenty of not-yet-household names. The museum also stages a number of temporary exhibits and career retrospectives each year, often focused on Scandinavian artists.

⊙ MAP P74, B2

☎ 08-52 02 35 00

www.modernamuseet.se

Exercisplan 4

admission free

⏱ 10am-8pm Tue & Fri, to 6pm Wed & Thu, 11am-6pm Sat & Sun

🅿

🚌 65, ⛴ Djurgårdsfärjan

1900s to 1940s

The galleries on the museum's main floor are arranged roughly by era, although things do tend to move around (and a large section is used for temporary exhibitions, usually with a separate admission fee). In the first of the permanent collection's three sections, you're likely to find early modernists like Edvard Munch and Ernst Ludwig Kirchner, Georgio de Chirico and several pieces by Marcel Duchamp.

Postwar to 1970s

Continuing through the main floor, you'll reach what are likely the most familiar names: Francis Bacon, Salvador Dalí, Robert Rauschenberg, Georges Braque and Pablo Picasso, plus an enormous and exuberant Henri Matisse cut-out covering one whole wall.

1970s to the Present

The farthest section usually holds the newest additions to the permanent collection, and as such is the most frequently changing. Things you might find here include Barbara Kruger paintings, Donald Judd installations, and envelope-pushing work by artists most of us haven't heard of yet, alongside important work by well-established Scandinavian artists.

Outdoor Sculptures

Arranged on the grounds around the museum are several sculptures by a wide variety of artists. The most attention-grabbing are the large colourful figures by Niki di Saint Phalle and Jean Tinguely, called *The Fantastic Paradise*. There's also an Alexander Calder and a Picasso, and work by several Swedish sculptors in the walled sculpture garden.

★ **Top Tips**

o Remember that the museum is closed on Mondays.

o Keep in mind that the permanent collection is rearranged frequently, and items from the collection are sometimes loaned out to other museums.

✕ **Take a Break**

There's a fabulous and very popular restaurant inside the museum with a great view over the water; an espresso bar in the foyer (next to the dreamy bookstore); and the small, casual **Cafe Blom**, a great place for lunch in a nice secluded courtyard.

Djurgården & Skeppsholmen Admire modern art at Moderna Museet

Walking Tour 🥾

Escape to Djurgården

In a perfect world, every city would have a place like Djurgården, a quiet, leafy green retreat from the noise and traffic of the working world. It is literally steps away from the heart of downtown Stockholm, but the park island feels like an otherworldly oasis. Part is occupied by Skansen and other excellent museums, but most consists of quiet trails through fields and forests, where locals exercise, picnic or just wander around.

Walk Facts

Start Djurgårdsbron, 🚋7
End Djurgårdsbron, 🚋7
Length 5.6km; two to three hours

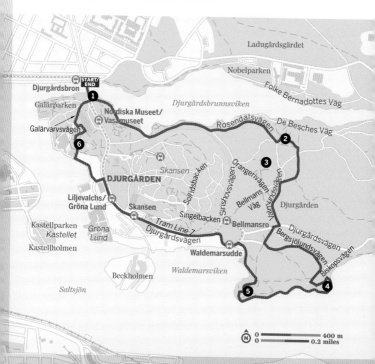

❶ Blue Gate

As soon as you walk across the bridge (Djurgårdsbron) from Norrmalm to Djurgården, you'll see a huge, bright-blue wrought-iron gate to your left. Walk through it and you'll be on the footpath alongside Djurgårdsbrunnsviken, the long stretch of water that separates the island from Ladugårdsgärdet to the north. Stay on the trail along the water's edge, stopping to admire baby ducks and passing boats as they appear.

❷ Rosendal

Eventually you'll reach signs pointing you towards **Rosendals Slott** (www.kungahuset.se; Rosendalsvägen 49; adult/child 100/50kr; ⏱hourly tours noon-3pm Tue-Sun Jun-Aug). Rosendal was built as a palace for Karl XIV Johan in the 1820s. One of Sweden's finest examples of the Empire style, it sparkles with sumptuous royal furnishings. Admission is by guided tour only – but even just the setting is well worth going to, and it's a handy landmark to orient yourself on the island.

❸ Botanical Gardens

The *trädgård* or botanical gardens attached to Rosendals Slott are well worth a look. They're designed as a forum for educating the public on the techniques and possibilities of organic gardening, but they're also just fun to wander through. You'll see everything from herbs and roses to vegetables and wine grapes – and of course an organic compost heap. King Oscar I built the orangery in 1848.

❹ Biskopsudden

This area sticks out a bit from the main island, which means it has excellent views across the water. There's a little cafe by the marina, **Cafe Ekorren** (www.cafeekorren. se; Biskopsvägen 5; mains 185-225kr; ⏱10am-8pm May-Sep), with outdoor tables beside the water as well as a little yellow hut for indoor seating. It's a great place to kick your feet up for a while and have a coffee, lunch or an ice cream.

❺ Waldemarsudde Garden Trails

The grounds around the highly recommended **Prins Eugens Waldemarsudde** (p77) gallery are equally well worth a visit – they're beautifully arranged, with multiple levels of walking paths and unexpected waterside gazebos that provide any number of picturesque views from different vantage points. Prins Eugen's grave is here, in a small, peaceful copse. Bring your camera and explore.

❻ Estonia Monument

As you wander back towards the bridge where the walk began, you'll pass the busy museums around Skansen. Take a small detour to visit the Estonia Monument. The structure commemorates the ferry disaster of 28 September 1994, in which 852 people drowned when a boat en route from Tallinn capsized in stormy weather.

Djurgården & Skeppsholmen

200 m
0.1 miles

De Besches Väg

Rosendalsterrassen

12 ✗

Rosendalsvägen

Orangerivägen

Sirishovsvägen

DJURGÅRDEN

Djurgårdsbrunnsviken

Skansen

Bellmansro

Solliddsbacken

Singelbacken

Valmundsvägen

Djurgårdsvägen

Prins Eugens väg

Djurgården

Prins Eugens
Waldemarsudde

8 ⊙

Waldemarsudde

Waldemarsviken

Tram Line 7
Djurgårdsvägen

Djurgårdsslätten

Skansen ⊙

Gröna

11 ⊙ Skansen

10 ⊙ Tändsticksmuseum

Tobaks &

Hazeliusporten

14 ✗

Nordiska Museet/
Vasamuseet

Liljevalchs/
Gröna Lund

13 ✗

4 ⊙

Gröna
Lund Tivoli

Gröna
Lund
Gränd

ABBA: The Museum

Lilla Allmänna
Gränd

Gröna
Lund

Beckholmen

Saltsjön

Narvavägen

Djurgårdsbron

Sjöcaféet

Visit Djurgården ⓘ

7 ⊙

Galärparken Nordiska
Museet

6 ⊙

Galärvarvsvägen

1 ⊙

Galärkyrkogården

Spritmuseum

2 ⊙

Vasamuseet

Junibacken

Slupskjulsvägen

Moderna
Museet ⊙

ArkDes

9 ⊙

Batteriparken

Exercisplan

Långa
Raden

Skeppsholmen

Svensksundsparken

Amiralitetsparken

Kastellparken

Kastellholmen

Tyghusparken

Ladugårdslandsviken

Tram Line 7

Styrmansgatan

Riddargatan

Strandvägen

Greygatan

Dag Hammarskjölds väg

Nobelgatan

Strömma

Kanalbolaget

5 ⊙

Strömmen

For reviews see	
⊙ Top Experiences	p64
⊙ Sights	p75
✗ Eating	p79

Sights

Nordiska Museet
MUSEUM

1 ⓞ MAP P74, C2

The epic Nordiska Museet is Sweden's largest cultural-history museum and one of its largest indoor spaces. The building itself (from 1907) is an eclectic, Renaissance-style castle designed by Isak Gustav Clason, who also drew up Östermalms Saluhall (p105); you'll notice a resemblance. Inside is a sprawling collection of all things Swedish, from sacred Sami objects to clothing and table settings. The museum boasts the world's largest collection of paintings by August Strindberg, as well as a number of his personal possessions. (☎08-51 95 47 70; www.nordiskamuseet.se; Djurgårdsvägen 6-16; adult/child 120kr/free; ⊘10am-5pm Sep-May, 9am-5pm rest of year, to 8pm Wed; 🚌44, 69, 🚢Djurgårdsfärjan, 🚋7)

Spritmuseum
MUSEUM

2 ⓞ MAP P74, C2

The surprisingly entertaining Museum of Spirits is dedicated to Sweden's complicated relationship with alcohol, as mediated over the years by the state-run monopoly System Bolaget. The slick space, in two 18th-century naval buildings, covers the history, manufacture and consumption of all kinds of booze, plus holiday traditions, drinking songs, food pairings

Forward Planning

For the big-ticket museums (ABBA, for example), it's best to buy tickets online, reserving a visiting time in advance.

and so on. Best of all, you can combine your visit with a tasting kit (250kr), including various flavours of liquor to be sampled at specified points. (Museum of Spirits; ☎08-12 13 13 00; www.spritmuseum.se; Djurgårdsvägen 38; adult/child 120kr/free; ⊘10am-5pm Mon, to 7pm Tue-Sat, noon-5pm Sun; 🚌44, 69, 🚢Djurgårdsfärjan, 🚋7)

Thielska Galleriet
GALLERY

3 ⓞ MAP P74, F3

Thielska Galleriet, at the far eastern end of Djurgården, is a must for Nordic art fans, with a savvy collection of late-19th- and early-20th-century works from Scandinavian greats like Carl Larsson, Anders Zorn, Ernst Josephson and Bruno Liljefors, plus a series of Edvard Munch's etchings of vampiric women and several paintings from a bridge you'll recognise from *The Scream*. (Ernest Thiel, a banker and translator, was one of Munch's patrons.) (☎08-662 58 84; www.thielska-galleriet.se; Sjötullsbacken 8; adult/child 130kr/free; ⊘noon-5pm Tue-Sun, to 8pm Thu; 🚌69)

Cashless Society

In typical ahead-of-the-curve Swedish style, Stockholm today is fast becoming a cashless society. Many businesses in the city, including several museums and major hotels, no longer accept payment by cash; debit or credit cards are considered safer. Payments by SMS are increasingly common too.

ABBA: The Museum   MUSEUM

4 ◉ MAP P74, C3

A sensory-overload experience that might appeal only to devoted ABBA fans, this long-awaited and wildly hyped cathedral to the demigods of Swedish pop is almost aggressively entertaining. It's packed to the gills with memorabilia and interactivity – every square inch has something new to look at, be it a glittering guitar, a vintage photo of Benny, Björn, Frida or Agnetha, a classic music video, an outlandish costume or a tour van from the band members' early days. (⏺08-12 13 28 60; www.abbathemuseum.com; Djurgårdsvägen 68; adult/child 250/95kr; ⏱9am-7pm Mon-Fri Jun-Aug, shorter hours rest of year; ⏹67, ⏴Djurgårdsfärjan, Emelie, ⏹7)

Strömma Kanalbolaget   BOATING

5 ◉ MAP P74, A1

This ubiquitous company offers tours large and small, from a 50-minute 'royal canal tour' around Djurgården (220kr) to a highly recommended 2¼-hour 'Under the Bridges of Stockholm' canal tour (280kr), the latter usually offered from mid-April to early November. There are also hop-on, hop-off tours by bus (from 320kr), boat (from 220kr) or both (from 450kr). (⏺08-12 00 40 00; www.stromma.se; Nybrohamnen)

Junibacken   AMUSEMENT PARK

6 ◉ MAP P74, B2

Junibacken whimsically recreates the fantasy scenes of Astrid Lindgren's books for children. Catch the flying Story Train over Stockholm, shrink to the size of a sugar cube and end up at Villekulla cottage, where kids can shout, squeal and dress up like Pippi Longstocking. The bookshop is a treasure trove of children's books, as well as a great place to pick up anything from cheeky Karlsson dolls to cute little art cards with storybook themes. (www.junibacken.se; Djurgården; adult/child 159/139kr; ⏱10am-6pm Jul-Aug, to 5pm rest of year; ⏹; ⏹44, 69, ⏴Djurgårdsfärjan, ⏹7)

Sjöcaféet

CYCLING

7 ⊙ MAP P74, C1

Rent bicycles from the small wooden hut below this restaurant, cafe and tourist-info centre beside Djurgårdsbron, Stockholm's centrally located bridge. It also offers canoes, kayaks and pedal boats for hire. Bring ID. (📞08-660 57 57; www.sjocafeet. se; Djurgårdsvägen 2; per hour/day bicycles 80/275kr, canoes 150/400kr, kayaks 125/400kr, pedal boats per hour 200kr; ⊙9am-9pm Jun-Aug, reduced hours rest of year; 🚌7)

Prins Eugens Waldemarsudde

MUSEUM

8 ⊙ MAP P74, E4

Prins Eugens Waldemarsudde, at the southern tip of Djurgården, is a soul-perking combo of water views and art. The palace once belonged to the painter prince (1865–1947), who favoured art over typical royal pleasures. In addition to Eugen's own work, it holds his impressive collection of Nordic paintings and sculptures, including works by Anders Zorn and Carl Larsson. The museum stages top-notch temporary exhibitions several times a year, usually highlighting the careers of important Scandinavian artists.

Djurgården & Skeppsholmen Sights

ABBA: The Museum

ROLF_52/SHUTTERSTOCK ©

On the Island

Jogging Stockholmers make excellent use of the running trails that lace Djurgården. Alternatively (you're on holiday, after all), this whole island is a picnicker's dream; bring a towel or blanket, a novel and a swimsuit to lounge away a sunny afternoon.

(📞 08-54 58 37 07; www.waldemar sudde.com; Prins Eugens väg 6; adult/child 150kr/free; ⏰ 11am-5pm Tue-Sun, to 8pm Thu, gardens 8am-9pm; 🚋 7)

ArkDes   MUSEUM

10 ⊙ MAP P74, B3

Adjoining Moderna Museet (p70) and housed in a converted navy drill hall, this architecture and design centre has a permanent exhibition spanning 1000 years of Swedish architecture and an archive of 2.5 million documents, photographs, plans, drawings and models. Temporary exhibitions also cover international names and work. The museum organises occasional themed architectural tours of Stockholm; check the website or ask at the information desk. (📞 08-58 72 70 00; www.arkdes.se; Exercisplan 4; special exhibits adult/child 120kr/free; ⏰ 10am-8pm Tue &

Fri, to 6pm Wed & Thu, 11am-6pm Sat & Sun; 🚌 65, 🚢 Djurgårdsfärjan)

Tobaks & Tändsticksmuseum   MUSEUM

10 ⊙ MAP P74, D3

Inside the vast open-air park of Skansen (p64), the Tobaks & Tändsticksmuseum traces the history and culture of smoking and the manufacture of those iconic Swedish matches. (Tobacco & Matchstick Museum; 📞 08-442 80 26; www.tobaksochtandsticksmuse um.se; admission free; ⏰ 11am-5pm, closed Mon Oct-Apr; 🚋 7)

Gröna Lund Tivoli   AMUSEMENT PARK

11 ⊙ MAP P74, C3

Crowded Gröna Lund Tivoli has some 30 rides, ranging from the tame (a German circus carousel) to the terrifying (the Free Fall, where you drop from a height of 80m in six seconds after glimpsing a lovely, if brief, view over Stockholm). There are countless places to eat and drink in the park, but whether you'll keep anything down is another matter entirely. The Åkband day pass gives unlimited rides, or individual rides range from 25kr to 75kr. (www.gronalund.com; Lilla Allmänna Gränd 9; entrance 115kr, unlimited ride pass 330kr; ⏰ 10am-11pm Jun-Aug, shorter hours rest of year; 🚼; 🚌 44, 🚢 Djurgårdsfärjan, 🚋 7)

Eating

Rosendals Trädgårdskafe

CAFE $$

12 ⊗ MAP P74, E2

Set among the greenhouses of a pretty botanical garden, Rosendals is an idyllic spot for heavenly pastries and coffee or a meal and a glass of organic wine. Lunch includes a brief menu of soups, sandwiches (such as ground-lamb burger with chanterelles) and gorgeous salads. Much of the produce is biodynamic and grown on-site. (✆08-54 58 12 70; www.rosendalstradgard.se; Rosen-dalsterrassen 12; mains 99-145kr; ⏱11am-5pm Mon-Fri, to 6pm Sat & Sun May-Sep, closed Mon Feb-Apr & Oct-Dec; Ⓟ 🐾; 🚌44, 69, 76 Djurgårdsbron, 🚋7)

Blå Porten Café

CAFE $$

13 ⊗ MAP P74, C3

This lovely cafe with a court-yard garden is located in the shadow of **Liljevalchs Konsthall**

(✆08-50 83 13 30; www.liljevalchs. se; Djurgårdsvägen 60; 🚌44, 69, 🚢Djurgårdsfärjan, 🚋7). (✆08-663 87 59; www.blaporten.com; Djurgårds-vägen 64; 🐾; 🚌47 Liljevalc Gröna Lund, 🚋7 Liljevalc Gröna Lund)

Wärdshuset Ulla Winbladh

SWEDISH $$$

14 ⊗ MAP P74, D2

Named after one of Carl Michael Bellman's lovers, this villa was built as a steam bakery for the Stockholm World's Fair (1897) and now serves fine food in inti-mate rooms and a blissful garden setting. Sup on skilfully prepared upscale versions of traditional Scandi favourites, mostly built around fish and potatoes – try the herring plate with homemade crispbread. (✆08-53 48 97 01; www.ullawinbladh.se; Rosendalsvägen 8; mains 175-425kr; ⏱11.30am-10pm Mon, 11.30am-11pm Tue-Fri, 12.30-11pm Sat, 12.30-10pm Sun; 🚢Djurgårdsfärjan, 🚋7)

Explore ◈

Södermalm

Slightly unvarnished and bohemian, Stockholm's southern island is where you'll find the coolest second-hand shops, art galleries, bars and espresso labs. The hills at the island's northern edge provide stunning views across Gamla Stan and the rest of the central city. A couple of museum heavyweights round out the to-do list, before taking in some of the city's most diverse nightlife.

The Short List

○ **Fotografiska (p82)** *Cutting-edge photography from around the world.*

○ **Tantolunden (p88)** *Adorable garden cottages on a park-adjacent hill.*

○ **Kvarnen (p90)** *Traditional beer hall that's the perfect place to sit with a pint.*

○ **Hermans Trädgårdscafé (p88)** *Line up for great vegetarian grub with a view.*

Getting There & Around

Ⓜ (Tunnelbana) Slussen, Medborgarplatsen, Hornstull, Skanstull, Mariatorget, Zinkensdamm

🚌 2, 3, 4, 53, 55, 57, 66, 71, 74, 94

Commuter rail (Pendeltåg) Stockholms södra

Neighbourhood Map on p86

Top Experience 📷

Appreciate photography at Fotografiska

A must for shutterbugs, the temporary exhibitions at this super-stylish museum are well curated and presented; examples have included Annie Leibovitz and Robert Mapplethorpe retrospectives. Fotografiska also offers photography courses, as well as staging occasional concerts and other one-off events. And it has one of the coolest locations in Stockholm.

◎ MAP P86, G3

www.fotografiska.eu

Stadsgårdshamnen 22

adult/child 135kr/free

🕑 9am-11pm Sun-Wed, to 1am Thu-Sat

🚇 Slussen

Temporary Exhibitions

In addition to its permanent collection, the museum holds four major temporary exhibitions a year, often in the form of retrospectives of big-name artists, as well as 15 to 20 smaller temporary exhibits. Memorable shows have featured enormous photos by Sebastião Salgado, an Irving Penn retrospective, and an exhibit of work by the Young Nordic Photographer of the Year, Akseli Valmunen. Others have included the likes of Annie Leibovitz, David LaChapelle, Klara Kallstrom and Johan Wik.

Film & Video

Some of the museum's temporary exhibitions incorporate short films and video, displayed on loops in small rooms tucked into various corners. Be sure to seek these out – it's often some of the most provocative and fascinating work in the gallery.

The Building

Fotografiska is housed in a massive (5500 sq metre) industrial art-nouveau brick structure designed by the well-known architect Ferdinand Boberg and built in 1906. It was originally a customs hall, and underwent a 250kr million renovation to transform the interior for the museum before opening in 2010.

Gift Shop

Plan to spend some time browsing the gift shop, as it's particularly well stocked. The collection of eccentric little cameras alone is interesting, but there are also hundreds of photos available to purchase and, of course, photography books, postcards and posters.

★ Top Tips

○ The Slussen area is set to be a construction zone for the next several years, so follow signs carefully from the tunnelbana station to reach the museum.

○ In the summer months, the terrace in front of the museum entrance becomes a lively bar and cafe serving cocktails and a brief menu of dinner specials and filling salads, usually with pumping DJ music in the background.

✖ Take a Break

The cafe on the museum's top floor serves coffee and cakes, decadent sandwiches and salads year-round, and the view from its panoramic windows is breathtaking.

Ready to leave the museum? Climb the stairs behind the building to Hermans Trädgårdscafe (p88) for a veggie buffet with a view.

Walking Tour 🥾

Bar-Hopping in Södermalm

It's a well-established fact that any neighbour-hood where artists and bohemian types live and work is a good place for a bar hop. In Stockholm, Söder is that neighbourhood, and the bars range from comfy dives to beautifully designed jewel boxes. The unifying factor, even in the coolest bars, is an unfussy open-mindedness. This part of town is all about fun.

Walk Facts

Start Medborgarplatsen
(🚇Medborgarplatsen)

End Tjärhovsgatan,
🚌66, 76

Length 7km; three to four hours

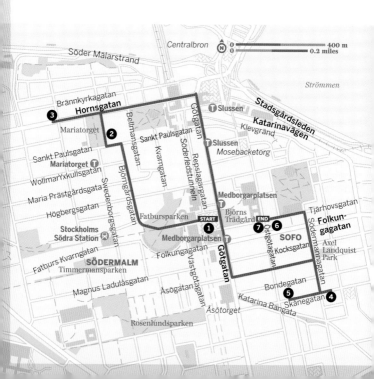

❶ Medborgarplatsen

At the edges of the vast open square that is Medborgarplatsen, all the bars in the area have roped-off outdoor seating. We recommend choosing a spot at whichever place offers the best eye candy.

❷ Mariatorget

Trek slightly northwest towards the lovely square Mariatorget, where you can enjoy a drink on the terrace or balcony of the ABBA-owned hotel **Rival** (☎08-54 57 89 24; www.rival.se; Mariatorget 3; ⏰5pm-midnight Thu-Sat).

❸ Marie Laveau

In an old sausage factory along Hornsgatan, **Marie Laveau** (www.marielaveau.se; Hornsgatan 66; ⏰5-11pm Mon & Tue, to 3am Wed-Sat) is a kicking Söder playpen that draws a boho-chic crowd. The designer-grunge bar (think chequered floor and subway-style tiled columns) serves killer cocktails, while the sweaty basement hosts club nights on the weekend. Known for its monthly 'Bangers & Mash' Britpop night – check online for a schedule.

❹ Snotty

Loop back towards the action: SoFo, south of Folkungagatan. Here you'll find **Snotty's** (Skånegatan 90; ⏰4pm-1am; 🚉Medborgarplatsen), a mellow hang-out that's friendly and free of attitude. It's one of the most comfortable and unpretentious places to drink in Stockholm. It has a vaguely retro vibe, a smooth wooden bar and record covers all over the walls.

❺ Bara Enkelt

Just down the street from Snotty's, decked out in shagalicious floral wallpaper and plush red sofas, **Bara Enkelt** (☎08-669 58 55; www.baras.se; Skånegatan 59; ⏰4pm-1am Mon-Fri, 3pm-1am Sat & Sun), formerly Bara Vi, is a popular hang-out for trendy 30-somethings who like their drinks list long and smooth. Check online for a schedule of indie rock acts on stage.

❻ Kebab Stop

Do as the locals do and stop for a greasy kebab at one of the carts on and around Medborgarplatsen – you'll need something to soak up all that adventure. For a sit-down version, try the friendly **Folkets Kebab** (☎08-669 91 66; Hornsgatan 92; buffet 119kr, kebabs from 50kr; ⏰10am-2am).

❼ On the Corner

Wrap up the tour with a last stop at one of the very few places you can find a cheap beer in the city: the little collection of dive bars at the corner of Tjärhovsgatan and Östgötagatan. What they lack in ambience they make up for in affordability, and you're bound to meet a lively crowd here.

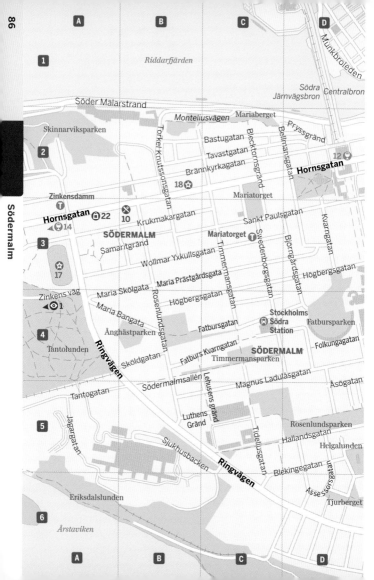

E

GAMLA STAN

Skeppsbron

F

G

H

N 0 ————————— 200 m
   0 ————————— 0.1 miles

1

For reviews see

⊙ Top Experiences   p82
⊙ Sights   p88
✖ Eating   p88
🍷 Drinking   p90
🎭 Entertainment   p91
🛍 Shopping   p93

Strömmen

Sjöbergsplan

Slussen
9 ✖

Slussen Ⓣ

Saltsjön

2

Södermalmstorg Stadsgårdshamnen
Katarinavägen   **Fotografiska** ⊙

Urvädersgränd 🅣🅣16 Klevgränd
15 Ⓣ Slussen 4
Mosebacketorg

Stadsgårdshamnen

Stadsgårdsleden

5 ✖ Fjällgatan

Lilla Erstagatan

Erstagatan

3

20 🛍 Högbergsgatan Mäster Mikaels Gata

Stigbergsgatan

Stigbergsparken

Stigbergsgatan

Tjärhovsplan

Medborgarplatsen Kapellgränd
Ⓣ Björns Trädgård
Medborgarplatsen Tjärhovsgatan
Ⓣ 11
Ⓣ Medborgarplatsen

Nytorgsgatan

Renstiernas Gata

Folkungagatan

Borgmästargatan

Beckbrännarbacken
Åsögatan

Klippgatan

Sågargatan

Bondegatan

4

SOFO
Kocksgatan 21🛍 Axel Landquist Park
19🛍 Östgötagatan ✖ 8 Lisa Larsson Second Hand
Bondegatan
Skånegatan

Söderledstunneln
13 🍷 ✖ 6
Götgatan Katarina Bangata Greta Garbos Torg
Turbergsgatan Nytorget ⊙ 2
⊙ 3

Vita Bergen

5

Blekingegatan ✖ 7

Sö/dermannagatan

Malmgårdsvägen

Allhellgonagatan Gotlandsgatan
Ⓣ Skanstull Bjurholmsplan
Ölandsgatan **Ringvägen**

Katarina Bangata

Ljusterögatan

Lilla Blecktornsparken

Skanstull Ⓣ

Stora Blecktornsparken

6

E F G H

Södermalm

Sights

Tantolunden
PARK

1 MAP P86, A4

Located in southwest Södermalm, adjacent to trendy Hornstull, Tantolunden is one of Stockholm's most extensive and varied parks. Its combination of allotments, open expanses, outdoor gym, play area and waterside walks make it a great getaway from the city centre. Although the park becomes a focal point of the city in the summer, with crowds flocking to swim and picnic, locals wind down with relaxing walks here throughout the year. (Zinkens Väg; Zinkensdamm, Hornstull)

Spårvägsmuseet
MUSEUM

2 MAP P86, H4

In a former bus depot near the Viking Line terminal, Stockholm's charmingly old-school transport museum is an atmospheric spot to spend a rainy afternoon. An impressive collection of around 40 vehicles includes several very pretty antique horse-drawn carriages, vintage trams and buses, and a retro tunnelbana carriage. Displays about the construction of the tunnelbana system starting in 1933 are pretty mind-blowing. (Transport Museum; 08-686 17 60; www.sparvagsmuseet.sl.se; Tegelviksgatan 22; adult/child 50/25kr; 10am-5pm Mon-Fri, 11am-4pm Sat & Sun; 2, 66 Spårvägsmuseet)

Leksaksmuseet
MUSEUM

3 MAP P86, H5

Sharing an entrance with Spårvägsmuseet, this toy museum is packed with everything you probably ever wanted as a child. If anybody in your family just happens to be crazy about model trains, toy soldiers, Barbie dolls or stuffed animals, don't miss it. (Toy Museum; 08-641 61 00; www.leksaksmuseet.se; Tegelviksgatan 22; adult/child 50/25kr; 10am-5pm Mon-Fri, 11am-4pm Sat & Sun; 2, 66 Spårvägsmuseet)

Eating

Woodstockholm
SWEDISH $$$

4 MAP P86, E3

Reservations are essential at this hip yet welcoming hotspot. The menu's theme changes every seven weeks or so, with a focus that ranges from specific geographic regions to more abstract concepts. What remains unchanging is a commitment to smaller, sustainable, local producers and honest, beautifully textured dishes cooked with flair. (08-36 93 99; www.woodstockholm.com; Mosebacketorg 9; mains 275-295kr; 5-11pm Tue-Sat; Slussen)

Hermans Trädgårdscafé
VEGETARIAN $$

5 MAP P86, G3

This justifiably popular vegetarian buffet is one of the nicest places to dine in Stockholm, with a glassed-in porch and outdoor seating on a terrace overlooking the city's glittering skyline. Fill up on inventive, flavourful veggie and vegan creations served from a cosy, vaulted room – you might need to muscle your way in, but it's worth the effort. (☏08-643 94 80; www.hermans.se; Fjällgatan 23B; buffet 195kr, desserts from 35kr; ☻11am-9pm; 🥗; 🚌2, 3, 53, 71, 76 Tjärhovsplan, 🚇Slussen)

Chutney
VEGETARIAN $$

6 🍴 MAP P86, F5

Sitting among a string of three inviting cafes along this block, Chutney is one of Stockholm's many well-established vegetarian restaurants, offering excellent value and great atmosphere. The daily lunch special is usually a deliciously spiced, Asian- or Indian-influenced mountain of vegies over rice, and includes salad, bread and coffee. (☏08-640 30 10; www.chutney.se; Katarina Bangata 19; daily special weekday/weekend 105/135kr; ☻11am-10pm Mon-Fri, noon-10pm Sat, noon-9pm Sun; 🥗; 🚇Medborgarplatsen)

Pelikan
SWEDISH $$$

7 🍴 MAP P86, F5

Lofty ceilings, wood panelling and no-nonsense waiters in waistcoats set the scene for classic *husmanskost* (home cooking) at this century-old beer hall – think roasted reindeer, Västerbotten cheese pie and Arctic char. The herring options are particularly

Kvarnen (p90)

Free Wi-fi

Right across Stockholm, wi-fi is almost always free and available at cafes, bus and train stations, hotels, hostels, 7-11 stores, ferries and on some trains.

good (try the 'SOS' starter, an assortment of pickled herring, 135kr to 195kr) and there's usually a vegetarian special. There's a hefty list of aquavit, too. (📞08-55 60 90 90; www.pelikan.se; Blekingegatan 40; mains 188-335kr; ⏰5pm-midnight or 1am; 🚇Skanstull)

String   CAFE $

8 ❌ MAP P86, G4

This retro-funky SoFo cafe does a bargain weekend brunch buffet (9am to 1pm Saturday and Sunday). Load your plate with everything from cereals, yoghurt and fresh fruit to pancakes, toast and amazing homemade hummus. Its daily lunch specials (lasagne, quiche) are good value, too. (📞08-714 85 14; www.facebook.com/cafestring; Nytorgsgatan 38; sandwiches 65-95kr, breakfast buffet 90kr; ⏰9am-10pm Mon-Thu, to 7pm Fri-Sun; 🚇Medborgarplatsen)

Nystekt Strömming   SWEDISH $

9 ❌ MAP P86, E2

For a quick snack of freshly fried herring, seek out this humble cart outside the tunnelbana station at

Slussen. Large or small combo plates come with big slabs of the fish and a selection of sides and condiments, from mashed potato and red onion to salads and crispbread; more-portable wraps and the delicious herring burger go for 55kr. (Södermalmstorg; mains 40-75kr; ⏰11am-9pm; 🚇Slussen)

Mahalo   VEGAN $$

10 ❌ MAP P86, B3

Fresh, colourful Mahalo celebrates all things vegan with a short, scrumptious selection of ecofriendly dishes. Top choices include the Buddha bowl, a fusion combo of tofu (or tempeh), greens, avocado, sour red cabbage, noodles, persimmon and sweet potato. There's also a virtuous soy burger, packed with vegan bacon, avocado, tomatoes, sambal and chilli mayo, and served with sweet potato fries.

Breakfast options are limited and include chia pudding. (📞08-42 05 65 44; www.mahalosthlm.se; Hornsgatan 61; mains 129-145kr; ⏰8am-7pm Mon-Fri, 10am-6pm Sat & Sun; 🛜✏️🐾; 🚇Mariatorget, Zinkensdamm)

Drinking

Kvarnen   BAR

11 🍺 MAP P86, E4

An old-school Hammarby football-fan hang-out, Kvarnen is one of the best (and best-loved) bars in Söder. The gorgeous beer hall dates from 1908 and seeps tradition; if you're not the clubbing type, get here early for a pint and a classic Swedish meal (mains from 225kr). As the night progresses, the nightclub vibe takes over. Queues are fairly constant but justifiable. (☎08-643 03 80; www.kvarnen.com; Tjärhovsgatan 4; ⏰11am-1am Mon & Tue, to 3am Wed-Fri, noon-3am Sat, noon-1am Sun; ⍰Medborgarplatsen)

Akkurat
BAR

12 🅔 MAP P86, D2

Valhalla for beer fiends, Akkurat boasts a huge selection of Belgian ales as well as a good range of Swedish-made microbrews and hard ciders. It's one of only two places in Sweden to be recognised by a Cask Marque for its real ale. Extras include a vast wall of whisky and live music several nights a week. (☎08-644 00 15; www.akkurat. se; Hornsgatan 18; ⏰3pm-midnight Mon, to 1am Tue-Sat, 6pm-1am Sun; ⍰Slussen)

Himlen
COCKTAIL BAR

13 🅔 MAP P86, E5

The only thing better than cocktails is cocktails on the 26th floor. While Himlen's cocktails mightn't be Stockholm's best crafted, they do come with spectacular views that make it a perfect spot for an afternoon or pre-dinner toast. The handful of wines by the glass include some interesting drops from Europe and well beyond, with decent bar bites including oysters. (☎08-660 60 68; www.restaurang-

himlen.se; 26th fl, Skrapan, Götgatan 78; ⏰11.30am-midnight Mon, to 1am Tue-Thu, to 3am Fri, noon-3am Sat; 🛜; ⍰Medborgarplatsen)

Debaser Strand
BAR

14 🅔 MAP P86, A3

Located in trendy Hornstull, Debaser is a Mexican restaurant, bar, nightclub and live-music venue all rolled into one big night out – it's a key draw to this area. The Brooklyn Bar is a comfy, unpretentious hang-out, with worn-in sofas and outdoor tables, and a good place to catch live music or DJ sets. (☎08-658 63 50; www.debaser.se; Hornstulls Strand 4; ⏰restaurant 5-11pm Tue-Thu, to 1am Fri & Sat, 11am-4pm Sun, bar Fri & Sat 4pm-3am; ⍰Hornstull)

Entertainment

Södra Teatern
THEATRE, LIVE MUSIC

15 ⭐ MAP P86, E3

Accessible from Mosebacketorg and adjoining Mosebacke Etablissement (p92), up the winding streets of old Södermalm, Södra Teatern is the original multifunctional event space, with its assortment of bars, stages and a restaurant. Whether you're relaxing in the beer garden or simply soaking up the ornate decor, this is a great place to dine and dance, or mingle with locals. Check the website for upcoming events. (☎08-53 19 94 90; www.sodrateatern. com; Mosebacketorg 1; ⏰8am-4pm Mon & Tue, to 11pm Wed & Thu, to 2am

Fri, 11.30am-2am Sat, noon-4pm Sun; ◎Slussen)

Mosebacke Etablissement

LIVE MUSIC

16 ⭐ MAP P86, E3

Eclectic theatre and club nights aside, this historic culture palace hosts a mixed line-up of live music. Tunes span anything from home-grown pop to Antipodean rock. The outdoor terrace (featured in the opening scene of August Strindberg's novel *The Red Room*) combines dazzling city views with a thumping summertime bar. It adjoins Södra Teatern and a couple of other bars. (http://sodrateatern. com; Mosebacketorg 3; ◎6pm-late; ◎Slussen)

Zinkensdamms Idrottsplats

SPECTATOR SPORT

17 ⭐ MAP P86, A3

Watching a bandy match is great fun. A precursor to ice hockey but with more players (11 to a side) and less fighting, the sport has grown massively popular since the rise of the Hammarby team in the late '90s. The season lasts from November to March; you can buy tickets at the gate. (www.svenskban dy.se/stockholm; Ringvägen 16; tickets around 130kr; ◎Zinkensdamm)

Folkoperan

THEATRE

18 ⭐ MAP P86, B2

Folkoperan gives opera a thoroughly modern overhaul with its intimate, cutting-edge

Mosebacke Etablissement

ROLF_52/SHUTTERSTOCK ©

and sometimes controversial productions. The under-26s enjoy half-price tickets. The attached restaurant-bar draws a loyal crowd on its own. (📞08-616 07 50; www. folkoperan.se; Hornsgatan 72; tickets 145-455kr; 🚇Zinkensdamm)

Shopping

English Bookshop BOOKS

19 🔒 MAP P86, F4

Excellent bookshop with second-hand and new titles, storytelling for kids, regular book signings (including Nell Zink of *The Wall-creeper* fame), writing workshops and plenty of seating space for perusing the pages. (📞08-790 55 10; Södermannagatan 22; ⏰10am-6.30pm Mon-Fri, to 5pm Sat, noon-3pm Sun; 🚇Medgorbarplatsen)

DesignTorget DESIGN

20 🔒 MAP P86, E3

If you love good design but don't own a Gold Amex, head to this chain, which sells the work of emerging designers alongside established denizens. There are several other locations, including one right next to the main tourist information office in Sergels Torg. (www.designtorget.se; Götgatan 31; ⏰10am-7pm Mon-Fri, 10am-6pm Sat, 11am-5.30pm Sun; 🚇Slussen)

Smiley Vintage VINTAGE

21 🔒 MAP P86, F4

This clever vintage shop remakes old clothes into new designs – no

Stockholm Vintage

A local fave among Söder-malm's stylish thrift shops (there are quite a few!), **Lisa Larsson Second Hand** (Map p86, G4; 📞08-643 61 53; Bondegatan 48; ⏰1-6pm Tue-Fri, 11am-3pm Sat; 🚇Medborgarplatsen) is a small space packed with treasures dating from the '30s to the '70s. Look for leather jackets, handbags, shoes and vintage dresses.

two items are alike. (Södermannagatan 14; ⏰11am-4.30pm Mon-Fri, 11.30am-5pm Sat, noon-4pm Sun; 🚇Medborgarplatsen)

Judits VINTAGE

22 🔒 MAP P86, A3

A highly curated and well-loved secondhand clothing store, Judits carries premier brands and organises them beautifully, creating the effect of a clothing museum. It's a fun place to browse even if your budget doesn't quite stretch far enough for a vintage Acne jacket. (📞08-84 45 10; www.judits. se; Hornsgatan 75; ⏰11am-6.30pm Mon-Fri, to 4.30pm Sat Sep-May, 11am-6pm Mon-Fri, to 4pm Sat Jun-Aug; 🚇Zinkensdamm)

Walking Tour 🥾

Water's Edge Walk

It's not for nothing Stockholm calls itself 'Beauty on Water'. The city is built across 14 islands and has miles of waterfront. This walk takes you along some of the best bits, with maximum postcard potential and a few key places to stop. It's best to do it in the late afternoon or early evening, and don't forget to bring a camera.

Walk Facts

Start Slussen

End Nybrokajen

Length 8km; one to three hours

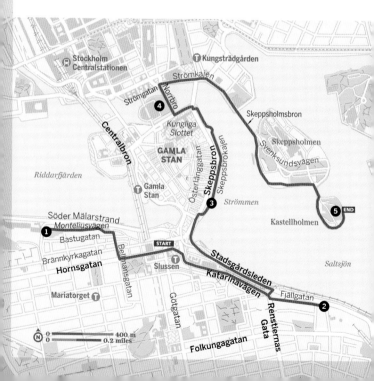

❶ Monteliusvägen

Follow Hornsgatan west from the Slussen tunnelbana stop; you'll pass **Akkurat** (p91), noteworthy as an excellent place to find good beer in Stockholm. Turn right at Bellmansgatan, then left at Bastugatan, which leads you to the tiny footpath called Monteliusvägen. This path extends through historic houses on one side, and on the other offers amazing views across the water and over the town.

❷ Fjällgatan

Cross back over the Slussen area and take Katarinavägen up the hillside, until it connects with Fjällgatan. This tiny street is the twin of Monteliusvägen – a gravel track through antique houses, it provides astounding views over the city from a slightly different angle. At its start/end point near **Hermans Trädgårdscafé** (p88) there's a rickety set of stairs leading down to the ground-level street, Stadsgårdsleden. Follow this back towards Slussen.

❸ Skeppsbrokajen

Stay next to the water as you walk across Gamla Stan, following Skeppsbron and Skeppsbrokajen. You'll see lots of boat traffic through here, and there's an uninterrupted view across the water (Strömmen) of Skeppsholmen.

❹ Strömparterren

Round the corner by the **palace** (p34) and turn right to walk across Norrbro. This small bridge, which crosses the sculpted park area known as Strömparterren, was nearly demolished to make way for a parking lot. Instead, thanks to some important underground discoveries, it now houses the excellent **Medeltidsmuseet** (p42). Follow the bridge and turn right, keeping to the water's edge as you walk alongside Norrström and onto the footbridge to Skeppsholmen.

❺ Kastellet

Walk along the westernmost edge of the parklike Skeppsholmen, passing by the famous floating youth hostel **Vandrarhem af Chapman & Skeppsholmen**. At the far end of the island is an even smaller islet, called Kastellholmen, where there's a fortress called Kastellet. Circle the edge of the islet for what is essentially a 360-degree, panoramic view of the surrounding areas, including Gamla Stan, Södermalm and Djurgården.

Explore ⊚
Östermalm

Östermalm is indisputably Stockholm's party district, where the beautiful, rich and famous come to play. It's also home to some of the city's best places to eat, drink and shop. But it isn't strictly about hedonism: this is also where you'll find two excellent history museums.

The Short List

o **Armémuseum (p104)** *Gaining an appreciation for the impact of war.*

o **Historiska Museet (p98)** *Wandering through 10,000 years of Sweden's past.*

o **Tekniska Museet (p111)** *Enjoying a fabulous place to be a kid, at any age.*

o **Naturhistoriska Riksmuseet (p104)** *Immersing yourself in natural history.*

Getting There & Around

Ⓜ (Tunnelbana) Östermalmstorg, Karlaplan, Stadion, Kungsträdgården

🚋 7, Nybroplan

🚌 1, 2, 54, 67, 68, 91, 96

Neighbourhood Map on p102

Dramaten (p107) ROLF_52/SHUTTERSTOCK ©

Top Experience 📷
Get to know the Vikings at Historiska Museet

Sweden's national historical collection awaits at this enthralling museum. From Iron Age skates and a Viking boat to medieval textiles and Renaissance triptychs, it spans over 10,000 years of Swedish culture and history. There's an exhibit about the Battle of Gotland (1361), an excellent multimedia display on the Vikings, a vast textile collection and a section on prehistoric culture.

◎ MAP P102, H4

☏ 08-51 95 56 20

www.historiska.se

Narvavägen 13-17

admission free

🕐 10am-5pm daily Jun-Aug, 11am-5pm Tue-Sun, to 8pm Wed Sep-May

🚌 67, 69, 76, 🚌 7, 🚇 Karlaplan, Östermalmstorg

Gold Room

The subterranean Gold Room is an undisputed highlight, a dimly lit chamber gleaming with Viking plunder and other treasures, including the jewel-encrusted Reliquary of St Elisabeth (who died at 24 and was canonised in 1235). The most astonishing artefacts are the three 5th-century gold collars discovered in Västergötland in the 19th century. The largest consists of seven rings, weighs 823g and is decorated with 458 symbolic figures.

Tapestries

The museum is known for its large collection of medieval textiles, including several that would have been displayed in very early wooden churches in northern Swedish villages.

Vikings

The museum's impressive Viking-era exhibition attempts to correct popular misconceptions about the Vikings and their age, focusing on their work as traders and on the lives of ordinary folk in those days (which, it turns out, was not all longboats and pillaging – most people were farmers). It's also a good place to learn about the rune stones that are still found scattered randomly across Sweden.

Battle of Gotland

One exhibit brings to life the medieval Battle of Gotland, which in 1361 pitted the island's farmers against professional soldiers in the Danish army. Needless to say it did not go well for the farmers: some 1800 were thrown into mass graves outside Visby. Archaeological studies have led to a clearer picture of what happened, and the display, though gruesome, is fascinating.

★ Top Tips

o The galleries are divided by era: the upper floor holds the Middle Ages and baroque, the main (ground) floor is dedicated to prehistory, while downstairs is the Gold Room, with treasures from prehistory to medieval times.

o Captions in English describe the treasures and displays, and offer insights into each item's history and how it was made.

✕ Take a Break

There's a coffee shop and cafe near the entrance, with pleasant courtyard seating during summer. For something outside the museum, head up Linnégatan for Thai food in a vivid setting at Sabai-Soong (p106).

Walking Tour 🥾

Opulent Östermalm

Östermalm has come quite a long way from its early days as a cattle field. Now one of the wealthiest areas of Stockholm, its elegant buildings, lush parks and classy shops make it a dream to wander through. The addresses in this part of town may be exclusive, but its beauty is here for everyone to enjoy.

Walk Facts

Start Humlegården,
🚌 1, 54, 75

End Strandvägen,
🚋 7, 🚌 69, 76,
Ⓣ Östermalmstorg

Length 2.8km, one to two hours

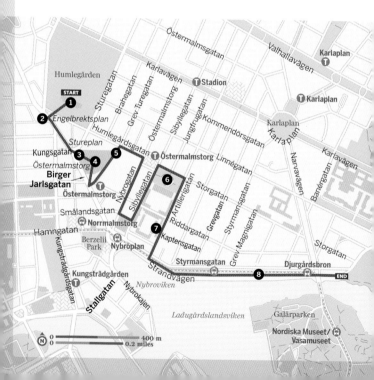

❶ Kungliga Biblioteket

Sweden's national library, Kungliga Biblioteket is beautifully situated in **Humlegården**, a leafy green park that acts as a neighbourhood oasis. The library holds a copy of virtually everything printed in Sweden or Swedish since 1661 (though it also has several much older items).

❷ Vassa Eggen

If you've started your day in the local fashion – that is, none too early – it's probably getting close to lunchtime. Treat yourself to the weekday lunch (145kr) at steakhouse **Vassa Eggen** (www.vassaeggen.com; Birger Jarlsgatan 29; ⏰11.30am-2pm Mon-Fri, 5.30-10pm Mon, to midnight Tue-Thu, to 2am Fri & Sat), a longstanding neighbourhood favourite.

❸ Svampen

Built in 1937, then smashed and rebuilt in the '80s, this oddball 'Mushroom' – originally meant to be rain protection – has become a landmark and one of the most popular places to meet people before heading out on the town.

❹ Sturegallerian

Home to dozens of high-end boutiques as well as the exclusive and historic spa **Sturebadet** (☎08-54 50 15 00; www.sturebadet.se; Sturegallerian 36, Stureplan; day pass from 595kr; ⏰6.30am-10pm Mon-Fri, 8.30am-8.30pm Sat & Sun), this is not your average shopping mall, with interiors built to blend with the 19th-century facade.

❺ Grev Turegatan

This pedestrianised shopping and dining street, along with Nybrogatan which runs parallel to the east, forms the core of the district – a highly concentrated dose of what Östermalm does best, with one-of-a-kind retail shops and sophisticated eateries set among beautiful apartment buildings.

❻ Hedvig Eleonora Kyrka

This pretty, octagonal **church** (www.hedvigeleonora.se; Storgatan 2; admission free; ⏰11am-6pm), consecrated in 1737, was initially designed by Jean de la Vallée in the 1660s as a private church for the Swedish Navy. The organ still has its original 1762 facade, by Carl Fredrik Aldencrantz. Check noticeboards for performance info.

❼ Kungliga Hovstallet

The 1894 Royal Stables occupy a red-brick building that extends for most of a block. The stables are part museum, part workplace – all royal-family transportation is arranged here, and the building holds 18 of the king's horses, as well as antique carriages and royal cars.

❽ Strandvägen

Probably the fanciest boulevard in the city, it also provides a stunning view across the water to the city skyline. Lined with proud houses sporting fairy-tale turrets, the street is nearly 80m wide, with a row of trees down the centre, making for quiet strolling.

A B C D

N 0 ———— 200 m
0 ———— 0.1 miles

1
2

Iversonsgatan
× 6

Birger Jarlsgatan

Jutas Backe

Rimbogatan

Engelbrektsgatan

16

Snickabacken

Humlegården

Karlavägen
Karlavägen

Kommendörsgatan

Sturegatan

Linnégatan

2

Engelbrektsplan

David Bagares Gata

Brunnsgatan

Humlegårdsgatan

Brahegatan

Grev Turegatan

Östermalmsgatan

Biblioteksgatan

12

3 ×

3

Kungsgatan

Norrlandsgatan

Stureplan

11

5 ×

Sturegallerian
Shopping
Centre

Östermalmstorg

Östermalmstorg

× 7

Regeringsgatan

Lästmakargatan

Jakobsbergsgatan

Stureplan

Östermalmstorg

15

1

4

Mäster Samuelsgatan

9 ×

Styckjunkargatan

Nybrogatan

Armémuseum

Sibyllegatan

Riddargatan

Smålandsgatan

Smålandsgatan

10

5

Hamngatan

Norrmalmstorg

Norrmalmstorg

Näckströmsgatan

13

Nybroplan

Berzelii
Park

14

Väpnargatan

Strandvägen

Kungsträdgårdsgatan

Berzelii
Park

Nybroplan

6

Kungsträdgården

Kockstorget
Kocksgränd

Kungsträdgården

Wahrendorffsgatan

Arsenalsgatan

Stallgatan

Nybroviken

A B C D

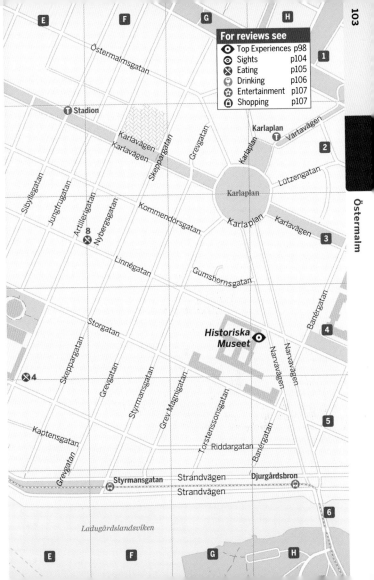

For reviews see

◉	Top Experiences	p98
◉	Sights	p104
✕	Eating	p105
🍷	Drinking	p106
✪	Entertainment	p107
🔒	Shopping	p107

Östermalmsgatan

🚇 Stadion

Karlaplan

Vartavägen

Karlavägen

Karlavägen

Skeppargatan

Grevgatan

Karlaplan

Lützengatan

Karlaplan

Sibyllegatan

Jungfrugatan

Artillerigatan

Nybergsgatan

Kommendörsgatan

Karlaplan

Karlavägen

⊗8

Linnégatan

Gumshornsgatan

Banérgatan

Storgatan

Historiska Museet ◉

Narvavägen

Skeppargatan

Grevgatan

Styrmansgatan

Grev Magnigatan

Narvavägen

⊗4

Torstenssonsgatan

Banérgatan

Kaptensgatan

Riddargatan

Grevgatan

Styrmansgatan

Strandvägen

Djurgårdsbron

Strandvägen

Ladugårdslandsviken

Sights

Armémuseum

MUSEUM

1 ⊙ MAP P102, D4

Delve into the darker side of human nature at Armémuseum, where three levels of engrossing exhibitions explore the horrors of war through art, weaponry and life-size reconstructions of charging horsemen, forlorn barracks and starving civilians. You can even hop on a replica sawhorse for a taste of medieval torture. (Artillery Museum; ☎08-51 95 63 00; www.armemuseum. se; Riddargatan 13; admission free; ⊙10am-7pm Jun-Aug, 11am-8pm Tue, to 5pm Wed-Sun Sep-May; ☒Öster-malmstorg)

Naturhistoriska Riksmuseet

MUSEUM

2 ⊙ MAP P102, A1

A fantastic place to bring kids, the Natural History Museum has seen a lot of changes since Carl von Linné founded it in 1739. These days, everything is interactive: you can crawl inside a human ear, sit through a forest fire or step into a chamber that mimics a swarm of mosquitoes. Of course, there are still countless displays of fossils, rock specimens, and whole forests' worth of taxidermied wildlife, marine life and the hardy fauna of the polar regions. (Swedish Museum of Natural History; ☎08-51 95 40 00; www.nrm.se; Frescativägen 40; admission free; ⊙10am-6pm Tue-Sun, open select Mon; P ♿; ☒Universitetet)

Armémuseum

JONATHAN SMITH/LONELY PLANET ©

Eating

Ekstedt   SWEDISH $$$

3 MAP P102, C3

Dining here is as much an experience as a meal. Chef Niklas Ekstedt's education in French and Italian cooking informs his approach to traditional Scandinavian cuisine – but only slightly. Choose from a four- or six-course set menu built around reindeer and pike-perch. Everything is cooked in a wood-fired oven, over a fire pit or smoked in a chimney. (📞08-611 12 10; http://ekstedt.nu/en; Humlegårdsgatan 17; 4/6 courses 890/1090kr; ⏰from 6pm till late Tue-Thu, from 5pm Fri, from 4pm Sat; 🚇Östermalmstorg)

Gastrologik   SWEDISH $$$

4 🍴 MAP P102, E4

Gastrologik is at the forefront of dynamic and modern Scandinavian cooking. Diners choose from a set three- or six-course menu, which changes frequently, as the chefs work closely with suppliers to deliver the freshest and most readily available produce with a nod to sustainability and tradition. Reservations are essential. (📞08-662 30 60; www.gastrologik.se; Artillerigatan 14; tasting menu 1595kr; ⏰6-11.30pm Tue-Fri, 5-11.30pm Sat; 🚇Östermalmstorg)

Sturehof   SEAFOOD $$$

5 🍴 MAP P102, B3

Superb for late-night sipping and supping, this convivial brasserie

Budget Bites

In need of a rapid-fire lunch that won't break the bank? The cafes and food counters inside **Östermalms Saluhall** (www.saluhallen.com; Östermalmstorg; ⏰9.30am-7pm Mon-Fri, to 5pm Sat; 🚇Östermalmstorg) make for an above-average yet still quick and generally budget-friendly lunch stop.

sparkles with gracious staff, celebrity regulars and fabulous seafood-centric dishes (the bouillabaisse is brilliant). Both the front and back bars are a hit with the eye-candy brigade and perfect for a postmeal flirt. (📞08-440 57 30; www.sturehof.com; Stureplan 2; mains 185-495kr; ⏰11am-2am; 🚇Östermalmstorg)

Café Saturnus   CAFE $

6 🍴 MAP P102, A1

For velvety caffè latte, Gallic-inspired baguettes and perfect pastries, saunter into this casually chic bakery-cafe. Sporting a stunning mosaic floor, stripy wallpaper and a few outdoor tables, it's a fabulous spot to flick through the paper while tackling what has to be Stockholm's most enormous sweet roll (cinnamon or cardamom, take your pick). (📞08-611 77 00; Eriksbergsgatan 6; sweet rolls 50kr, salads & sandwiches 68-138kr; ⏰8am-8pm Mon-Fri, 9am-7pm Sat & Sun; 🚌2 Eriksbergsgatan)

Lisa Elmqvist

SEAFOOD $$$

7 MAP P102, D3

Lisa Elmqvist is somewhat of an institution in Stockholm, famed for its fresh, gorgeous seafood dishes. Classics include shrimp sandwiches and a gravadlax plate, though it's always worth scanning the blackboard for the day's handful of specials. If you're undecided, trust the waitstaff's recommendations. Quality extends to the well-versed wine list. (08-55 34 04 10; www.lisaelmqvist.se; Östermalms Saluhall, Östermalmstorg; mains from 245kr; 11am-10pm Mon & Tue, to 11pm Wed-Sat; Östermalmstorg)

Sabai-Soong

THAI $$

8 MAP P102, F3

Super-kitsch Sabai-Soong is keeping it real despite the snooty address. A hit with families and fashionistas alike, its tropical-trash day-glo interior is the perfect place to chow down on simple and faithful versions of *tod man pla* and fiery green curry. (08-663 12 77; www.sabai.se; Linnégatan 39B; 11am-2pm Mon-Fri, 5-10pm daily; Östermalmstorg)

Sturekatten

CAFE $

9 MAP P102, C4

Looking like a life-size doll's house, this vintage cafe is a fetching blend of antique chairs, oil paintings, ladies who lunch and servers in black-and-white garb. Slip into a salon chair, pour some tea and nibble on a piece of apple pie or a *kanelbulle* (cinnamon bun). (08-611 16 12; www.sturekatten. se; Riddargatan 4; pastries from 35kr; 9am-7pm Mon-Fri, 9am-6pm Sat, 10am-6pm Sun; Östermalmstorg)

Drinking

Lilla Baren at Riche

BAR

10 MAP P102, C5

A darling of Östermalm's hip parade, this pretty, glassed-in bar mixes smooth bar staff, skilled DJs and a packed crowd of fashion-literate media types; head in by 9pm to score a seat. (08-54 50 35 60; Birger Jarlsgatan 4; 5pm-2am Tue-Sat; Östermalm)

Sturecompagniet

CLUB

11 MAP P102, C3

Swedish soap stars, flowing champagne and look-at-me attitude set a decadent scene at this glitzy, mirrored and becurtained hallway. Dress to impress and flaunt your wares to commercial house. Big-name guest DJs come through frequently. (08-54 50 76 00; www.sturecompagniet.se; Stureplan 4; 10pm-3am Thu-Sat; Östermalmstorg)

Spy Bar

CLUB

12 MAP P102, B3

Though it's no longer the super-hip star of the scene it once was, the Spy Bar (aka 'the Puke'; *spy* means vomit in Swedish) is still a landmark and fun to check out if you're making the Östermalm rounds. It covers three levels in a turn-of-the-century flat (spot the tile stoves). (Birger Jarlsgatan 20; cover from 160kr; ⏰10pm-5am Wed-Sat; 🚇Östermalmstorg)

Entertainment

Dramaten
THEATRE

13 ⭐ MAP P102, C5

The Royal Theatre stages a range of plays in a sublime art-nouveau environment. You can also take a guided tour in English at 4pm most days (adult/child 30/60kr), bookable online. Half-price tickets may be available an hour before showtime, for those willing to gamble. (Kungliga Dramatiska Teatern; 📞08-667 06 80; www.dramaten.se; Nybroplan; tickets 150-450kr; 🚇Kungsträdgården)

Shopping

Svenskt Tenn
ARTS, HOMEWARES

14 🅐 MAP P102, D5

As much a museum of design as an actual shop, this iconic store is home to the signature fabrics and furniture of Josef Frank and his contemporaries. Browsing here is a great way to get a quick handle on what people mean by 'classic Swedish design' – and it's owned by a foundation that contributes heavily to arts funding. (📞08-670 16 00; www.svenskttenn.se; Nybrogatan 15; ⏰10am-6pm Mon-Fri, 10am-4pm Sat; 🚇Kungsträdgården)

Nocturnal Scenes

The streets branching off from Östermalmstorg hold some of the city's primo nightclubs as well as mellower terrace bars – ideal for a bit of people-watching.

Nordiska Galleriet
ARTS & CRAFTS

15 🅐 MAP P102, D4

This sprawling showroom is a design freak's El Dorado – think Hannes Wettstein chairs, Hella Jongerius sofas, Alvar Aalto vases and mini Verner Panton chairs for style-sensitive kids. Luggage-friendly options include designer coathangers, glossy architecture books and bright Marimekko paper napkins. (📞08-442 83 60; www.nordiskagalleriet.se; Nybrogatan 11; ⏰10am-6pm Mon-Fri, to 5pm Sat; 🚇Östermalmstorg)

Rönnells Antikvariat
BOOKS

16 🅐 MAP P102, A2

From vintage Astrid Lindgren books to dusty 19th-century travel guides, the 100,000-strong collection of books here, many in English, make this one of the meatiest secondhand bookshops in town. Forage through the sales rack for a new dog-eared friend. (📞08-54 50 15 60; www.ronnells.se; Birger Jarlsgatan 32; ⏰10am-6pm Mon-Fri, noon-4pm Sat; 🚇Östermalmstorg)

Worth a Trip 🔭
Enter the world of Carl Milles at Millesgården

From 1906 to 1931, Millesgården was the home and studio of sculptor Carl Milles (1875–1955), whose delicate water sprites and other whimsical sculptures dot the city. The artist's delightful personality, which is clearly evident in his sculptures, also imbues the house where he lived and worked. It's an inspiring place to visit, especially for anyone interested in art and design.

📞 08-446 75 90

www.millesgarden.se

Herserudsvägen 32

adult/child 150kr/free

🕐 11am-5pm, closed Mon Oct-Apr

🚇 Ropsten, then bus 201, 202, 204, 206, 207

Art Gallery

The grounds include a crisp modern gallery in neoclassical style for changing exhibitions of contemporary art. Carl and Olga Milles themselves laid the tiles for the intricate black-and-white mosaic floor.

Sculpture Park

Milles transformed the rough hillside of the property into an exquisite outdoor sculpture garden, where items from ancient Greece, Rome, medieval times and the Renaissance intermingle with his own creations. Seek out 'Little Austria', a garden space Milles designed for his wife to ease her homesickness. Most of the garden is arranged to evoke the Mediterranean coast.

Little Studio

Inside the sculpture park, the Little Studio, built by Milles' brother Evert, contains a fresco painting of the Bay of Naples. Black-and-white marble paths bordered by pines and birches, and crowned with Italianate columns, lead the way to the studio. The studio was initially built to improve the state of Milles' lungs, which suffered from the dust his work created.

Milles' Home

The artist couple visited Pompeii in 1921, and after this trip they started adding elaborate Pompeiian touches to the decor – especially in what became the Red Room, with its mosaic floors and frescoed walls. Olga painted the kitchen cabinets after the Delft ceramic-tiled walls. The Music Room contains not only a grand piano but also a Donatello sculpture and a Canaletto painting, among other treasures.

★ **Top Tips**

o From mid-June through August, a 30-minute guided introduction in English is included in the ticket price, starting at 1.15pm Tuesday and Thursday.

o Be sure to bring a good camera – the setting is very photogenic.

✗ **Take a Break**

The **Millesgården Lanthandel** (mains 155-220kr) cafe and restaurant occupies the middle terrace of the Sculpture Park. It serves coffee, cakes, lunch and dinner either outdoors or inside by the fireplace in winter.

★ **Getting There**

Millesgården is on the island of Lidingö, northeast of the city.

Tunnelbana Ropsten, then bus 207.

Worth a Trip Enter the world of Carl Milles at Millesgården

Walking Tour 🥾

Museums of Gärdet & Ladugårdsgärdet

These two conjoined parklike areas – one a casual suburban neighbourhood, the other a former royal playground that's now a wide-open green space – contain some of the best museums in the city. And they're much easier to reach than they may initially seem – a quick bus or tunnelbana trip, or a leisurely walk from Östermalm.

Getting There

Gärdet and Ladugårdsgärdet are east of Östermalm.

🚇 Gärdet

🚌 69 from Kaknästornet

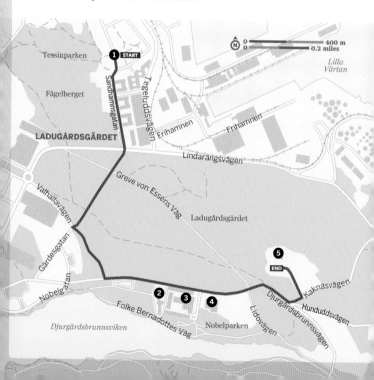

❶ Gärdet Tunnelbana Station

From the Gärdet tunnelbana station, walk south along Sandhamnsgatan through a quiet residential neighbourhood and onto the wide open field that is Ladugårdsgärdet. This is a great place for a picnic or a nap in the sun, or a jog if you're more ambitious.

❷ Sjöhistoriska Museet

At the southern edge of Ladugårdsgärdet, you'll find a trio of excellent kid-friendly museums. The smallest and cutest of the three is the nautical **Sjöhistoriska Museet** (National Maritime Museum; ☏08-519 549 00; Djurgårdsbrunnsvägen 24; admission free; ◷10am-5pm Tue-Sun) – a must for fans of model ships (there are over 1500 mini vessels in the collection). The exhibits also explore Swedish shipbuilding, sailors and life on deck.

❸ Tekniska Museet

Tekniska (Museum of Science & Technology; ☏08-450 56 00; www.tekniskamuseet.se; Museivägen 7; adult/child 150/100kr, free 5-8pm Wed; ◷10am-5pm Thu-Tue, to 8pm Wed; 🚋; 🚌69 Museiparken) is a vast museum full of interactive science and technology displays. You can test your balance, flexibility and strength with the kinetic experiments and exhibits in the huge 'Teknorama' room, and the museum also features a climate-change game, a model railway and an exhibition dedicated to inventions by women.

❹ Etnografiska Museet

Next door, the fascinating and atmospheric **Museum of Ethnography** (☏010-456 12 99; www.etnografiska.se; Djurgårdsbrunnsvägen 34; admission free; ◷11am-5pm Tue-Sun, to 8pm Wed) stages evocative displays on various aspects of non-European cultures, including dynamic temporary exhibitions and frequent live performances. Recent examples include a display about the cultural treasures of Afghanistan, a look at gender norms, and 'real-life' voodoo. There's a good cafe, too.

❺ Kaknästornet

It's a nice walk to reach the big lookout tower that looms over this whole area. The 155m-tall Kaknästornet is the automatic operations centre for radio and TV broadcasting in Sweden. Opened in 1967, it's among the tallest buildings in Scandinavia. There's a small visitor centre on the ground floor and an elevator up to the observation deck, restaurant and cafe near the top, from where there are stellar views of the city and archipelago.

Explore ⊛
Kungsholmen

Until recently something of an underappreciated gem, especially among visitors, Kungsholmen has really come into its own. This is a laid-back, mostly residential neighbourhood with great places to eat, kid-friendly parks and an amazingly long stretch of tree-lined waterside walking. Plus it's home to one of Stockholm's most important buildings, architecturally and practically, in Stadshuset (City Hall).

The Short List

○ **Stadshuset (p114)** Taking in the water views from City Hall.

○ **Bergamott (p117)** Having a fabulous French-inspired meal.

○ **Rålambshovsparken (p117)** Getting a swim or an outdoor workout in.

○ **Mälarpaviljongen (p118)** Dining on a floating restaurant.

Getting There & Around

Ⓜ (Tunnelbana) Rådhuset, Fridhemsplan

🚌 1, 3, 4, 54, 56, 61, 65, 91

🚶 It's a short walk across Stadshusbron from the area around Centralstationen

Neighbourhood Map on p116

TUPUNGATO/SHUTTERSTOCK ©

Top Experience 📷
Tour the mighty Stadshuset

The City Hall dominates Stockholm. It looks stern and weighty from afar, but inside it's secretly aglitter. Built of about eight million bricks, it was designed by architect Ragnar Östberg, a proponent of the Swedish National Romantic style, and opened in 1923. Aside from serving as a striking landmark, it holds the offices of more than 200 government workers.

◉ MAP P116, F4

www.stockholm.se/stadshuset

Hantverkargatan 1

adult/child 100/50kr, tower 50kr/free

🕑 9am-3.30pm, admission by tour only

🚌 3, 62 Stadshuset,
🚇 Rådhuset

The Tower

Atop the building's 106m-high tower is a golden spire featuring the heraldic symbol of Swedish power: the three royal crowns. Entry is by guided tour only; tours in English take place every 30 to 40 minutes between 9.30am and 4pm in summer, less frequently the rest of the year. There are stellar views and it's a great thigh workout.

Golden Hall

Nestled in the centre of Stadshuset is the glittering, mosaic-lined *Gyllene salen* (Golden Hall; pictured left). The beguiling mosaics, made from 19 million bits of gold leaf, are by Einar Forseth (1892–1988). The post-Nobel banquet dancing and festivities happen here.

Prins Eugen's Fresco

Prins Eugen, who became a successful artist and was a generous patron of the arts, donated his own fresco painting of the lake view from the gallery, *The City on the Water,* which can be seen along one wall in the Prince's Gallery. Along the other wall are windows opening on to an impressive real-life version of the city on the water.

Stadshusparken

Don't neglect the lovely park abreast of Stadshuset, pretty in all seasons, with its views of Riddarholmen across the water. Two statues by Carl Eldh guard the steps, and Christian Eriksson's *Engelbrekt* the *Freedom Fighter* graces a pillar in the corner of the park. If the weather's warm, do as Stockholmers do and take a swim or sunbathe on the concrete platform.

★ Top Tips

○ Note that the tower and tower museum are only open for visits from May through September.

○ If you're not sure you're up for walking 106m worth of stairs, there's an elevator that will take you halfway to the top.

✕ Take a Break

You can dine like a Nobel Prize winner in Stadshuset's basement restaurant, **Stadshuskällaren** (www.stadshuskallarensthlm.se). Regular mains (285kr to 310kr) are mostly hearty traditional meat-and-veg courses; groups can order the Nobel Menu (1865kr) from any year they like, served on Nobel porcelain. Reservations are recommended.

Kungsholmen

NORRMALM

T-Centralen 🚇

Stockholm
Centralstationen

Stadshuset

Stadshusbron

Klarastrandsleden

Kungsbron

Kungsbro
Strand

Klara Sjö

Kaplansbacken

Norr Mälarstrand

Kungsbron

Kungsholmsgatan

Scheelegatan

Piperssgatan

Kungsgatan

Klarabergsviadukten

Parmmätargatan

Rådhuset 🚇

Hantverkargatan

Garvargatan

Kungsholmstorg

Barnhusbron

Kungsholmsstrandsstig

Kungsholms Strand

Torsgatan

Barnhusviken

Norra Agnegatan

Fleminggatan

Sankt Eriks
ögonsjukhus

Polishuset

Rådhuset

Bergsgatan

Pilgatan

Landstingshuset 2 ✕

Sankt
Eriksbron

Kungsholms
Strand

Kungsholmsstrand

Inedalsgatan

Parkgatan

Kronobergsparken

Polhemsgatan

Kronobergsgatan

Hantverkargatan

5 🛈

Pontonjärparken

Pontonjärgatan

Pontonjärgatan

Norr Mälarstrand

✕ 3

Sankt Eriksbron

Fridhemsplan

Industrigatan

Alströmergatan

Arbetargatan

Mariebergsgatan

6 🍷

Fridhemsgatan

Fridhemsplan 🚇

Fridhemsplan

Drottningholmsvägen

7 🛈

Fridhemsplan

Hantverkargatan

Karlviksgatan

Sankt Eriksgatan

Fridhemsgatan

Kronobergsgatan

Smedsuddsvägen

Rålambshovsleden

Rålambshovsparken

1 ◎

Stadshagen

Welanders Väg

Sankt Göransgatan

Riddarfjärden

500 m
0.25 miles

Sights

Rålambshovsparken   PARK

1 MAP P116, A3

In the warmer months, Rålamb-shovsparken is one of the city's favourite playgrounds, packed with picnicking Swedes fresh from a dip in the lake. Take a swim, hire a canoe or just get physical at the free alfresco fitness sessions. Rålambshovs-parken is the place to join locals in whatever the latest exercise trend may be: outdoor yoga, aerobics, crossfit, bootcamp...you name it, they're into it. And there's nearly always a nightly exercise class of some kind through the summer. (🚇Fridhemsplan)

Eating

Bergamott   FUSION $$$

2 🍽 MAP P116, D3

The very cool French chefs in this kitchen don't simply whip up to-die-for French-Italian dishes, they'll probably deliver them to your table, talk you through the produce and guide you through the wine list. It's never short of a convivial crowd, so it's best to book, especially when jazz musicians drop in for a soulful evening jam. Menu changes daily. (📞08-650 30 34; www.restaurang bergamott.se; Hantverkargatan 35; mains 195-325kr; 🕐5.30pm-midnight Tue-Sat; 🚇Rådhuset)

Lemon Bar (p118)

Street Eats

There are plenty of interesting places to eat in Kungsholmen, but you'll find a particularly good and varied range of eateries along **Scheelegatan** and **Hantverkargatan**, where the two streets intersect. Kungsholmen is a great area for exploring unpretentious neighbourhood restaurants, small cafes and ethnic cuisines – follow your nose, or the crowds. And as always in Stockholm, the people-watching/admiration here is part of the street experience.

Mälarpaviljongen

SWEDISH, AMERICAN $$

3 🟢 MAP P116, C4

When the sun's out, few places beat this alfresco waterside spot for some Nordic dolce vita. Its glassed-in gazebo, vast floating terraces and surrounding herb gardens are only upstaged by the lovely and supremely welcoming service. Both food and cocktails are beautified versions of the classics: meatballs, fried herring, gravadlax and the like. Opening times vary with the weather. (📞08-650 87 01; www.malarpa viljongen.se; Norr Mälarstrand 63; mains 185-225kr; ⏲11am-1am; 🚇Rådhuset)

Drinking

Lemon Bar

BAR

4 🚇 MAP P116, D3

A favourite among locals for its laid-back vibe, the Lemon Bar epitomises the kind of comfy neighbourhood joint you can drop into on the spur of the moment and count on finding a friendly crowd and good music, mostly Swedish pop hits that may or may not result in dancing. (📞08-650 17 78; www.lemonbar.se; Scheelegatan 8; ⏲5pm-1am Tue, to 3am Wed-Sat; 🚇Rådhuset)

Shopping

59 Vintage Store

VINTAGE

5 🔒 MAP P116, C3

This rack-packed nirvana of retro threads will have you playing dress-up for hours. Both girls and boys can expect high-quality gear from the 1950s to the 1970s, including glam, midcentury ball-gowns, platform boots, Brit-pop blazers, *Dr Zhivago* faux-fur hats and the odd sequinned sombrero. (📞08-652 37 27; www.59vintagestore. se; Hantverkargatan 59; ⏲11am to 6pm Mon-Fri, 11am-4pm Sat; 🚇Råd-huset)

Grandpa

ACCESSORIES, CLOTHING

6 🔒 MAP P116, B1

With a design inspired by the hotels of the French Riviera during the '70s, Grandpa's second

Viking
History

Scandinavia's greatest impact on world history probably occurred during the Viking Age (late 8th into the mid-11th century) when hardy pagan Norsemen set sail for other shores. The Swedish Vikings were more inclined towards trade than their Norwegian or Danish counterparts, but their reputation as fearsome warriors was fully justified. At home it was the height of paganism; Viking leaders claimed descent from Freyr, 'God of the World', and celebrations at Uppsala involved human sacrifices.

Long-Distance Raiders

The Vikings sailed fast manoeuvrable boats, sturdy enough for ocean crossings. Initial hit-and-run raids along the European coast were followed by military expeditions, settlement and trade. The Vikings visited the Slavic heartland (giving it the name 'Rus'), and ventured as far as Newfoundland, Constantinople (Istanbul) and Baghdad.

Christianity Arrives

Christianity only took hold when Sweden's first Christian king, Olof Skötkonung (c 968–1020), was baptised. However, by 1160, King Erik Jedvarsson (Sweden's patron saint, St Erik) had virtually destroyed the last remnants of Viking paganism.

In a Word

The word 'Viking' is derived from *vik*, meaning bay or cove – probably a reference to Vikings' anchorages during raids. The root word appears in many Swedish place names – Örnsköldsvik, in northern Sweden, for example; or Alvik, a Stockholm tunnelbana stop.

Learn More about the Vikings

The Vikings by Magnus Magnusson covers their achievements in Scandinavia (including Sweden), as well as their wild deeds around the world. The Viking trading centre of **Birka** (www.birkavikingastaden. se/en; adult/child 395/198kr; ☉May-Sep; ⛴Stromma), on Björkö in Lake Mälaren, makes a fantastic day trip. A Unesco World Heritage site, it was founded around 760 CE to expand and control trade in the region. It now offers an up-close look at Viking history. **Strömma Kanalbolaget** (www.stromma.se) runs cruises.

Essential Swedish Books and Films

One of the best ways to get inside the collective mind of a country is to read its top authors – here's a Swedish fiction primer:

Popular Works

Famous books by Swedish authors include *The Long Ships* (1954) by Frans Gunnar Bengtsson, *The Wonderful Adventures of Nils* (1906–07) by Selma Lagerlöf, the *Emigrants* series (1949–59) by Vilhelm Moberg, *Marking* (1963–64) by Dag Hammarskjöld, *Röda Rummet* (1879) by August Strindberg, *The Evil* (1981) by Jan Guillou and, more recently, *A Man Called Ove* (2013) by Fredrik Backman.

Crime Fiction

It's the country's detective fiction that has drawn the most attention recently, however. The massive success of the Millennium Trilogy, by the late Stieg Larsson, has brought well-deserved attention to the genre. *The Girl with the Dragon Tattoo* (2005) is the tip of the iceberg when it comes to this genre.

Other names to look for include Håkan Nesser, whose early novels *The Mind's Eye* (1993) and *Woman with Birthmark* (1996) have recently been translated into English; and Sweden's best-known crime fiction writer, Henning Mankell, whose novels featured moody detective Kurt Wallander. Johan Theorin's quartet of mysteries (starting with *Echoes from the Dead*, 2008) is set on the island of Öland. Other writers include Karin Alvtegen (Sweden's 'queen of crime'), Kerstin Ekman, Camilla Läckberg and Jens Lapidus.

Film

One man has largely defined modern Swedish cinema to the outside world: Ingmar Bergman. With deeply contemplative films such as *The Seventh Seal*, *Through a Glass Darkly* and *Persona*, the beret-topped director explored human alienation, the absence of God, the meaning of life, the certainty of death and other light-hearted themes.

More recently, the Swedish towns of Trollhättan and Ystad have become filmmaking centres, the former drawing the likes of director Lukas Moodysson, whose *Lilja 4-Ever*, *Show Me Love* and *Tillsammans* were popular and critical hits. Moodysson's newest film, 2014's *We Are the Best!*, is an uplifting movie about three high-schoolgirls in 1980s Stockholm who form a punk band out of spite.

Stockholm location is crammed with atmosphere, as well as artfully chosen vintage and faux-vintage clothing, cool and quirky accessories and whatnots, random hairdryers, suitcases and old radios, plus a cool little cafe serving good espresso. (📞08-643 60 81; www.grandpa.se; Fridhemsgatan 43; ⏰11am-7pm Mon-Fri, to 5pm Sat, noon-4pm Sun; 🚇Fridhemsplan)

Västermalmsgallerian

SHOPPING CENTRE

7 🔒 MAP P116, B1

This busy mall right outside the Fridhemsplan tunnelbana stop is home to some noteworthy residents. Pick up Scandi-design wares at DesignTorget, sexy Swedish briefs at BjörnBorg, cult cosmetics at Face Stockholm, and democratically priced kids' and women's threads at H&M. (📞08-737 20 00; www.vastermalmsgallerian. se; St Eriksgatan 45; ⏰10am-7pm Mon-Fri, to 5pm Sat, 11am-5pm Sun; 🚇Fridhemsplan)

Urban Beaches

Kungsholmen boasts the largest beach in the Stockholm city centre, called **Smed-suddsbadet**. At the first sign of warm weather in spring, locals flock here to soak up the sun after the long, dark Swedish winter. To find the beach, follow the footpath along Norr Mälarstrand west beside the water towards **Rålambshovs-parken** (p117).

Don't be afraid to explore Kungsholmen on foot – the island is not as big as one might think, and on two feet you're more likely to discover unexpected things around corners. Besides, with all those Swedish meatballs you'll be consuming, you're going to need to burn off a few surplus calories every day.

Worth a Trip 🔭

Visit the royal residence at Drottningholm

The royal residence and parks of Drottningholm on Lovön are justifiably popular attractions and easy to visit from the capital. Home to the royal family for part of the year, Drottningholm's Renaissance-inspired main palace was designed by architectural great Nicodemus Tessin the Elder and begun in 1662, about the same time as Versailles.

📞 08-402 62 80

www.kungahuset.se

adult/child 130/65kr, combined ticket incl Kina Slott 190/90kr

🕐 10am-4.30pm May-Sep, 11am-3.30pm Oct & Apr, noon-3.30pm Sat & Sun rest of year (closed mid-Dec–Jan)

Hedvig Eleonora's Bedchamber

The highly ornamented State Bedchamber of Hedvig Eleonora (1636–1715), consort of King Karl X Gustav, is Sweden's most expensive baroque interior (pictured left). It's decorated with paintings featuring the childhood of their son, who would become King Karl XI. The painted ceiling shows the queen consort with her king.

Karl X Gustav Gallery

The Karl X Gustav Gallery, in baroque style, depicts this monarch's militaristic exploits – though the paintings on the ceiling are of classical battle scenes, lending their mythical heft to Karl X's persona.

Library

Although the bulk of Queen Lovisa Ulrika's collection of 2000 books has been moved to the Royal Library in Stockholm for safekeeping, her library here is still a bright and impressive room, complete with most of its original 18th-century fittings.

Corps de Garde

The Lower North Corps de Garde was originally a guard room, bare and functional, but as the need for armed guards just outside the door diminished, this room was repurposed and beautified. It's now replete with gilt-leather wall hangings, which used to feature in many palace rooms during the 17th century.

Staircase

The palace's elaborate staircase, with statues and trompe l'œil embellishments at every turn, was the work of both of the Nicodemus Tessins, the Elder and the Younger. From the landing you can gaze out at the gardens, of a similarly clever geometrical design angled to impress. Filled with fountains and labyrinths, these are well worth exploring.

★ **Top Tips**

Explore on your own, or take a one-hour guided tour (30kr; in English at 10am, noon, 2pm and 4pm June to August, noon and 2pm other months).

✕ **Take a Break**

Bring a picnic and enjoy lunch in the gardens, or munch at one of the restaurants by the palace. **Cafe Drottningholm** (📞 08-759 03 96; Kantongatan; waffles 65kr; ⏰ 9am-4.30pm May-Sep) is a cute cafe next to Kina Slott.

★ **Getting There**

Drottningholm is 10km west of Stockholm.

Bus/Metro T-bana to Brommaplan, then bus 176 or 177 to Drottningholm.

Boat Strömma Kanalbolaget boats from Stadshuskajen.

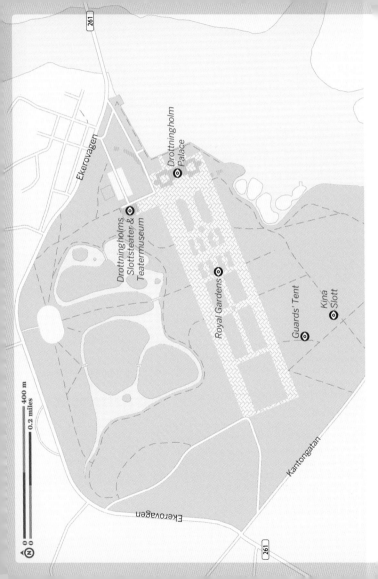

261

Ekerövägen

Drottningholm
Palace

Drottningholms
Slottsteater &
Teatermuseum

Royal Gardens

Guards' Tent

Kina
Slott

Kantongatan

Ekerövägen

261

400 m
0.2 miles

N

Visit the royal residence at Drottningholm

Drottningholms Slottsteater & Teatermuseum

Completed in 1766, **Slottsteater** (Court Theatre & Museum; www.dtm. se; entry by tour adult/child 100/70kr; ⏰ tours hourly noon-3.30pm Fri-Sun Oct & Apr, noon-3.30pm Sat & Sun Nov & Mar, 11am-4.30pm May-Aug, 11am-3.30pm Sep) was built on the instructions of Queen Lovisa Ulrika. Remarkably untouched from the time of Gustav III's death (1792) until 1922, it's now the oldest theatre in the world still in its original state. The fascinating guided tour takes you into other rooms in the building, where highlights include hand-painted 18th-century wallpaper and an Italianate room (salon de déjeuner) with fake three-dimensional wall effects and a ceiling that looks like the sky.

Performances are held at Drottningholms Slottsteater in summer using 18th-century machinery, including ropes, pulleys, wagons and wind machines that allow scenes to be changed in less than seven seconds. Illusion was the order of the day, and accordingly the theatre makes use of fake marble, fake curtains and papier-mâché viewing boxes.

Kina Slott

At the far end of the royal gardens is **Kina Slott** (Chinese Pavilion; adult/child 100/50kr, combined ticket incl royal palace 190/90kr; ⏰11am-4.30pm May-Sep), a lavishly decorated Chinese pavilion built by King Adolf Fredrik as a birthday surprise for Queen Lovisa Ulrika in 1753. Restored between 1989 and 1996, it boasts one of the finest rococo chinoiserie interiors in Europe. Admission includes guided tours, which run at 11am, 1pm and 3pm daily from June to August (fewer in May and September).

Guards' Tent

On the slope below Kina Slott, the carnivalesque Guards' Tent was erected in 1781 as quarters for the dragoons of Gustav III, but it's not really a tent at all. The building now has displays about the gardens and Drottningholm's Royal Guard.

Hedvig Eleonora

The queen consort of King Karl X Gustav, Hedvig Eleonora was by all accounts a great beauty and a strong leader. After the king's death in 1660, she became regent until their son, Karl XI, came of age. When he died in 1697, she returned to that position, but only briefly, until her grandson, Karl XII, became king. Both son and grandson were devoted to Hedvig Eleonora and took her counsel seriously. Hers was an age of intrigue and gossip, rumoured affairs and various sordid alliances, both personal and political. She loved the theatre, had a gambling habit and liked to party.

Explore ◈

Vasastan

This relaxed, residential neighbourhood has some of the best places to eat in Stockholm, along with several great hotels and a couple of slick art galleries in impressive buildings. It's also home to one of the greatest examples of Scandinavian architecture, Stadsbiblioteket. Wander around, take a nap in a park and join the laid-back locals in just hanging out.

The Short List

○ **Stadsbibliotek (p129)** *Admiring the fine lines of the library building.*

○ **Bonniers Konsthall (p129)** *Checking out adventuresome new works of art.*

○ **Sven-Harrys Konstmuseum (p129)** *Exploring a gallery in a design-forward building.*

○ **Strindbergsmuseet (p129)** *Studying the life of the beloved and bedevilled author.*

○ **Tranan (p130)** *Indulging in a traditional meal at this upscale neighbourhood spot.*

Getting There & Around

Ⓜ (Tunnelbana) St Eriksplan, Odenplan, Rådmansgatan

🚌 2, 3, 4, 6, 50, 53, 67, 72, 96

Neighbourhood Map on p128

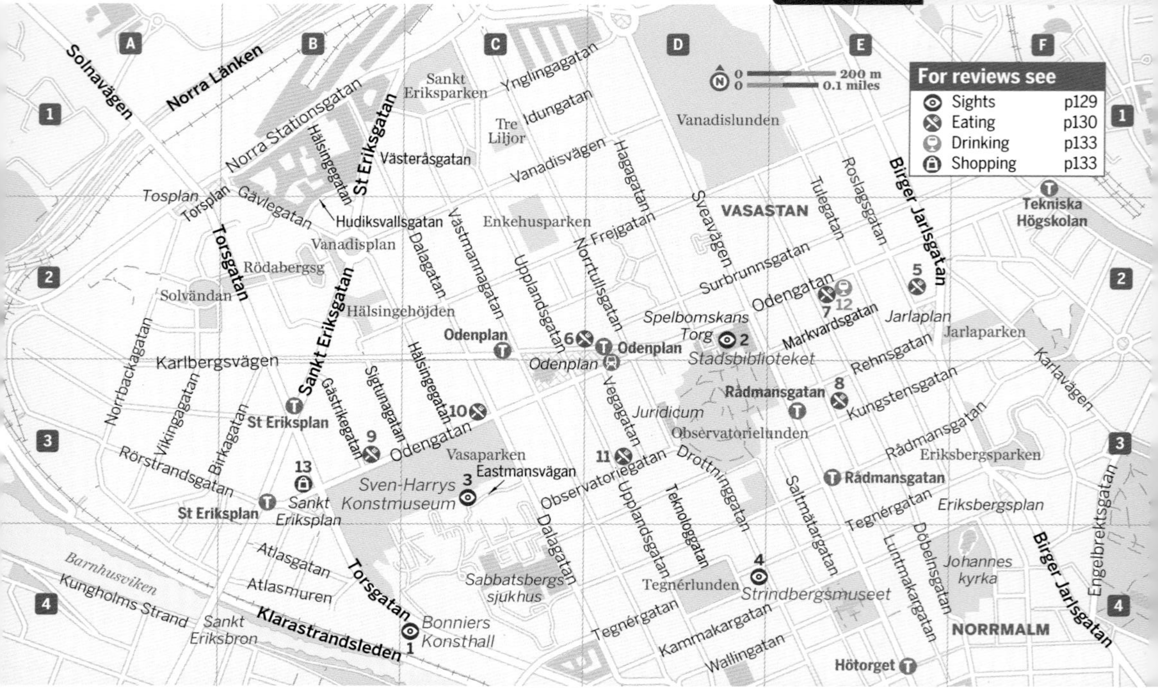

For reviews see
Sights p129
Eating p130
Drinking p133
Shopping p133
0 200 m
0 0.1 miles
A
B
C
D
E
F
1
2
3
4
Solnavägen
Norra Länken
Norra Stationsgatan
Hälsingegatan
St Eriksgatan
Västeråsgatan
Sankt Eriksparken
Ynglingagatan
Tre Liljor
Idungatan
Vanadisvägen
Vanadislunden
Hagagatan
Tosplan
Torsplan
Gävlegatan
Hudiksvallsgatan
Torsgatan
Vanadisplan
Enkehusparken
Frejgatan
Norrtullsgatan
Sveavägen
VASASTAN
Tulegatan
Roslagsgatan
Birger Jarlsgatan
Tekniska Högskolan
Rödabergsg
Solvändan
Dalagatan
Västmannagatan
Upplandsgatan
Surbrunnsgatan
Odengatan
5
7
12
Hälsingehöjden
Sankt Eriksgatan
Odenplan
6
Spelbomskans Torg
2
Markvardsgatan
Jarlaplan
Jarlaparken
Karlbergsvägen
Stadsbiblioteket
Rehnsgatan
Karlavägen
Norrbackagatan
Gästrikegatan
Sigtunagatan
Hälsingegatan
10
Rådmansgatan
8
Kungstensgatan
St Eriksplan
Juridicum
Vegagatan
Observatorielunden
Vikingagatan
Birkagatan
9
Vasaparken
11
Drottninggatan
Rådmansgatan
Eriksbergsparken
Rörstrandsgatan
13
Eastmansvägan
Sven-Harrys Konstmuseum
3
Observatoriegatan
Sankt Eriksplan
Teknologgatan
Saltmätargatan
Tegnérgatan
Eriksbergsplan
Engelbrektsgatan
Atlasgatan
Atlasmuren
Sabbatsbergs sjukhus
4
Tegnérlunden
Strindbergsmuseet
Luntmakargatan
Döbelnsgatan
Johannes kyrka
Barnhusviken
Kungholms Strand
Sankt Eriksbron
Klarastrandsleden
Bonniers Konsthall
1
Kammakargatan
Wallingatan
Hötorget
NORRMALM

Sights

Bonniers Konsthall   GALLERY

1 ◉ MAP P128, C4

This ambitious gallery keeps culture fiends busy with a fresh dose of international contemporary art, as well as a reading room, a fab cafe and a busy schedule of art seminars and artists-in-conversation sessions. The massive, transparent flatiron building was designed by Johan Celsing. There are discussions about the exhibitions in English at 1pm, 3pm, 5pm and 7pm on Wednesday, and 1pm and 4pm Thursday to Sunday. Curators lead free guided tours on Sunday at 2pm. (📞08-736 42 48; www.bonnierskonsthall.se; Torsgatan 19; admission free; ⊙noon-5pm Thu-Sun, to 8pm Wed; 🚇St Eriksplan)

Stadsbiblioteket   LIBRARY

2 ◉ MAP P128, D2

The main city library is just north of the city centre. Designed by architect Erik Gunnar Asplund and sporting a curvaceous, technicolor reading room, it's the finest example of Stockholm's 1920s neoclassicist style. (📞08-50 83 10 60; Sveavägen 73; admission free; ⊙10am-7pm Mon-Fri, noon-4pm Sat; 🚇Odenplan)

Sven-Harrys Konstmuseum   MUSEUM

3 ◉ MAP P128, C3

This ultramodern building houses an art gallery with interesting

Park Life

Hang out in the amazing, multifaceted **Vasaparken**, a huge park that runs alongside Odengatan and has al fresco exercise options, a running track, football pitches, quiet places to read and a giant playground where kids can run wild.

temporary exhibitions (recently a collection of August Strindberg's paintings, borrowed from Strindbergsmuseet), as well as a recreation of the former Lidingö home of owner and art collector Sven-Harry Karlsson. Access to the home is by guided tour (150kr, 45 minutes, currently in Swedish only). There's also an award-winning restaurant with terrace seating facing the park. (📞08-51 16 00 60; www.sven-harrys.se; Eastmansvägen 10-12; adult/child 100kr/free; ⊙11am-7pm Wed-Fri, to 5pm Sat & Sun; 🚇Odenplan)

Strindbergsmuseet   MUSEUM

4 ◉ MAP P128, D4

The small but evocative Strindbergsmuseet in the Blue Tower is the well-preserved apartment where writer and painter August Strindberg (1849–1912) spent his final four years. Visitors can peep into his closet, scan his study and library (containing some 3000 volumes), do a round of the dining room and take in the often

Affordable Fine Dining

At high-end restaurants you can sample fine dining on a more reasonable budget by ordering the daily lunch special, wherever you decide to eat – it's usually a great choice anyway, but also comes with salad, bread and coffee.

absorbing temporary exhibits. (☏08-411 53 54; www.strindbergs museet.se; Drottninggatan 85; adult/child 75/50kr; ☒Rådmansgatan)

Eating

Caffé Nero   CAFE $$

5 ✖ MAP P128, E2

Packed with local hipsters during the busy lunch hour, this stylish but casual neighbourhood cafe serves substantial Italian meals (fish, pasta, salads) at good prices, plus sublime coffee and pastries. Next door is a more formal bar-restaurant, Buco Nero, with DJs most nights. (www.nerostockholm.se; Roslagsgatan 4; lunch mains 110-145kr; dinner mains 145-175kr; ☺7am-4pm Mon-Fri, 9am-5pm Sat & Sun; ☒Odenplan, Rådmansgatan)

Tranan   SWEDISH $$$

6 ✖ MAP P128, C2

Locals pack this former beer hall, now a comfy but classy neighbourhood bistro with a seafood-heavy menu and chequered tablecloths.

The food combines Swedish *husmanskost* (home cooking) with savvy Gallic touches; don't miss the fried herring. In summer, choose an outdoor table and watch the human dramas across Odenplan. On the weekends, DJs and live bands perform in the basement bar. (☏08-52 72 81 00; www.tranan.se; Karlbergsvägen 14; mains 160-395kr; ☺11.30am-11pm Mon-Fri, noon-11pm Sat & Sun, 5-11pm daily Jul & Aug; ☒Odenplan)

Storstad   FRENCH, SWEDISH $$$

7 ✖ MAP P128, E2

This attractive bistro near Odenplan, which shares a corner (and owners) with Olssons bar (p133), serves Scandi classics like *toast skagen* or Swedish meatballs alongside traditional French favourites like *moules frites* and tarte Tatin. It transforms into a lively cocktail bar later in the evening. (www.storstad.se; Odengatan 41; plates 125-325kr; ☺4pm-1am Mon-Wed, to 3am Fri & Sat; ☒Odenplan)

Lao Wai   VEGETARIAN $$$

8 ✖ MAP P128, E3

Tiny, herbivorous Lao Wai does great things to tofu and vegetables, hence the faithful regulars. Everything here is gluten-free and vegan. A different Asian-fusion lunch special is served each weekday; the dinner menu is more expansive, offering virtuous treats like Sichuan-style smoked tofu with shiitake, chillies, garlic shoots, snow peas and black beans.

THORIR INGVARSSON/SHUTTERSTOCK ©

Stadsbiblioteket (p129)

(☎08-673 78 00; www.laowai.se; Lunt-makargatan 74; dagens lunch 110kr, dinner mains 220-240kr; ⊙11am-2pm Mon-Fri, 5.30-9pm Mon-Sat; 🖊; 🚇Rådmansgatan)

Vurma   CAFE $$

9 ❌ MAP P128, B3

This comfy cafe is part of a chainlet of restaurants and serves filling, healthy salads, soups, curries and sandwiches. (www.vurma. se; Gästrikegatan 2; mains 99-139kr; ⊙11am-8pm; 🖊; 🚇St Eriksplan)

Konditori Ritorno   CAFE $

10 ❌ MAP P128, C3

The cosy backroom at this un-presumptuous cafe looks like the lobby of an old movie house fallen on hard times. A hit with writers,

students and pensioners, its worn leather couches and miniature jukeboxes at every table make it a perfect pit stop for old-school shrimp sandwiches and heavenly *semla* buns. (☎08-32 01 06; Odengatan 80-82; sandwiches from 50kr; ⊙7am-10pm Mon-Thu, to 8pm Fri, 8am-6pm Sat, 10am-6pm Sun; 🚇Odenplan)

Flippin' Burgers   BURGERS $$

11 ❌ MAP P128, D3

Part of Stockholm's current obsession with burgers, FB has a brief menu (just a few types of burger, fries and shakes) and a perpetual line out the front door. But things move quickly; squeeze into the bar for a Sam Adams beer while you wait. Burgers are simple and delicious, relying on

Eating in Stockholm

Sweden has come a long way from the days of all-beige fish and potato platters. Not only has immigration and membership in the EU introduced new flavours to the Swedish menu, a new wave of bold young chefs has been experimenting with traditional Swedish fare and melding it with various other influences. The result is an exciting dining scene on a par with some of the best food cities in Europe.

Classic Cuisine

Traditional Swedish cuisine is based on simple, everyday ingredients known generally as *husmanskost*, or basic home cooking. The most famous example of this, naturally, is Swedish meatballs. Other classic *husmanskost* dishes, largely based around fish and potatoes, include various forms of pickled and fried herring, cured salmon (gravlax) and *pytt i panna*, a potato hash served with sliced beets and a fried egg on top that may be the ultimate comfort food. Open-face shrimp sandwiches are everywhere, piled high with varying degrees of art and mayonnaise. Of course, the most thorough introduction to all the staples of Swedish cooking is the smörgåsbord, commonly available during the winter holidays.

Modern Menus

Essentially, contemporary Swedish cuisine melds global influences with local produce and innovation. Locals have rediscovered the virtues of their own pantry, alongside the more intense flavours arriving in Sweden from abroad. The result is a great passion for seasonal, home-grown ingredients, whether apples from Kivik or bleak roe from Kalix, used in creative new ways. Equally important is the seasonality of food: expect succulent berries in spring, artichokes and crayfish in summer, and hearty truffles and root vegetables in the colder months. Alongside this appreciation for the cycles of farming has come a newfound reliance on sustainable, small-scale farmers and organic produce. Increasingly, restaurants and cafes pride themselves on serving organically grown and raised food, as well as actively supporting ethical, eco-friendly agricultural practices.

high-quality ingredients (sustainably raised beef, ground in-house daily). (📞08-30 62 40; http://flippinburgers.se/en; Observatoriegatan 8; burger 95-130kr, fries 35kr; 🕐4-10pm Mon-Thu, 11am-10pm Fri, noon-10pm Sat & Sun; 🚇Odenplan)

Drinking

Olssons skor   BAR

12 🚇 MAP P128, E2

The blue neon sign outside this bar tips you off to its former life as a shoe store. These days, it serves as the back bar to Storstad (p130), forming a busy corner of activity along this neighbourhoody street. (📞08-673 38 00; Odengatan 41; 🕐9pm-3am Wed-Sat; 🚇Odenplan)

Shopping

Cajsa Warg   FOOD

13 🔒 MAP P128, B3

A gourmet food store that focuses on sustainable products and a tranquil, pleasant shopping atmosphere, Cajsa Warg is fun to browse but also makes for a mean picnic basket if you're so inclined. Pick up gift boxes and souvenir treats to take home. (📞08-33 01 20; www.cajsawarg.se; St Eriksplan 2; 🕐8am-8pm Mon-Fri, 10am-7pm Sat & Sun, open later in summer; 🚇St Eriksplan)

Who's for a Beer?

There are plenty of casual neighbourhood pubs and corner bars around Vasastan. The pick of the bunch is probably **Tennstopet** (📞08-32 25 18; www.tennstopet.se; Dalagatan 50; dagens lunch 129kr; 🕐11.30am-1am Mon-Fri, 1pm-1am Sat & Sun; 🚇Odenplan): had there been a Swedish version of *Cheers,* it would've been filmed here.

As much a place to eat as it is to drink, this atmospheric local haunt is festooned with oil paintings and gilded mirrors, winter candlelight setting the scene for a loveable cast of wizened regulars, corner-seat scribes and melancholy dames.

Watch the show with a soothing *öl* (beer) and a serving of soulful *husmanskost*. Try the traditional herring platter for two (196kr).

Worth a Trip 👀

Get on the water in the Archipelago

Mention the archipelago to Stockholmers and prepare for gushing adulation. Buffering the city from the Baltic Sea to the east, it's a wonderland of rocky isles with forests and wildflowers, dotted with wooden cottages (pictured). Exactly how many islands there are is debatable, but the general consensus is 24,000. It's unmissable and much closer to the city than many visitors imagine.

The archipelago's gateway is road-accessible Vaxholm, 35km northeast of Stockholm.

🚢 Waxholmsbolaget (www.waxholmsbolaget. se) is the main ferry operator; single trips cost 47–130kr

Vaxholm

There are plenty of reasons to visit Vaxholm, the most obvious being that it is the closest archipelago island to Stockholm (there's even a bridge – you can catch a bus here). The island offers a charming taster of this extraordinarily diverse area; on a sunny spring day, its crooked streets and storybook houses are irresistible. **Hembygdsgård** (☏08-54 13 19 80; Trädgårdsgatan 19; admission free; ☺museum noon-4pm Fri-Mon Jun, to 4pm Fri-Sun Jul & Aug, cafe 11am-5pm Sat & Sun May, to 5pm daily Jun-early Sep) is a museum preserving some of these fine old homes. Vaxholm has a thriving restaurant scene, including the landmark Waxholms Hotell (p135). For baked goodies, try **Boulangerie Cafe** (☏08-54 13 18 72; www.boulangerie.se; Soderhamnen 6; pastries from 25kr, dishes 65-145kr; ☺6.30am-6.30pm Mon-Fri, to 7pm Fri, 8am-6pm Sat; ☎). There's a helpful **tourist office** (☏08-54 13 14 80; www.vaxholmdestination.se; Rådhuset; ☺10am-6pm Mon-Fri, to 4pm Sat & Sun Jun-Aug, shorter hours rest of year) here, too.

Utö

Star of the archipelago's southern section, Utö has it all: sublime sandy beaches; lush forests; sleepy farms; abundant birdlife; an awesome organic bakery, **Utö Bageri** (☏070-015 19 00; Gruvbryggan; pastries from 25kr, lunch from around 140kr, sandwiches 45-80kr; ☺7am-5pm); and a highly rated restaurant, **Nya Dannekrogen** (☏08-50 15 70 79; www.nyadannekrogen.se; Bygatan 1; mains 195-315kr, pizzas 120-155kr; ☺noon-1am daily mid-Jun–Aug, reduced hours rest of year; 🅿🚻). Utö's network of level roads and trails make for heavenly cycling sessions; ask at the **tourist office** (☏08-50 15 74 10; www.uto.se/en/uto-tourist-office; Gruvbryggan; ☺10am-6pm Jun-Aug) about cycle hire. The best sandy beach is **Stora Sand** on the south coast. Gruvbryggan, the island's northernmost village, is the main ferry stop. **Utö Vårdshus** (☏08-50 42 03 00;

★ **Top Tips**

◦ Waxholmsbolaget divides the archipelago into three sections: middle, north and south. Within each section, several numbered routes go out and back, usually once a day, calling at various ports along the way.

◦ Keep in mind that most island villages are remote, with limited options for dining and groceries; bring some provisions along. There are also bar-restaurants on the boats.

✗ **Take a Break**

You're likely to end up in Vaxholm on any archipelago journey, either to change ferries or just strolling around to enjoy the pretty harbour town. While you're here, head to the historic **Waxholms Hotell** (☏08-54 13 01 50; www.waxholmshotell.se; Hamngatan 2; buffet 415kr, mains 180-315kr; ☺noon-10.30pm Mon-Sat, to 6pm Sun) for a scrumptious seafood meal.

Fast or Slow?

There are essentially two ways to visit the archipelago, depending on your preferred travel style.

If time is short, take an organised boat tour of anywhere from a few hours to a full day, passing several islands and making brief stops at one or two. Check with Strömma Kanalbolaget (p76) for options that suit you – the most thorough option is the popular 'Thousand Islands' day tour (from 1235kr), which includes lunch and dinner and takes in parts of the outer archipelago.

Otherwise, you can plan your own longer, slower, self-guided trip using **Waxholmsbolaget** (☎08-600 10 00; www.waxholmsbolaget.se; Strömkajen; ⏰7am-2pm Mon, 8am-2pm Tue-Thu, 7.30am-4.30pm Fri, 8am-noon Sat, 8.30am-noon Sun; 🚇Kungsträdgården) services with overnight stays. The area's many comfortable hostels, campsites and cushy hotels – plus some excellent restaurants – make the latter option dreamy if you have a few days to spare, though it does take a bit more planning.

www.utovardshus.se; Gruvbryggan; r hostel/hotel from 690/1600kr; 🛜) is the island's only hotel/hostel.

Arholma

Arholma is a quiet, idyllic island in the archipelago's far north. Practically everything here was burnt down during a Russian invasion in 1719. The landmark lighthouse was rebuilt in the 19th century and is now an art gallery with impressive views. The entire island is a nature reserve, with hiking trails, cycle paths, kayaking routes, sandy beaches and even a forest zip line. The excellent **STF Arholma/Bull-August Gård** (☎0176-560 50; www.bullaugust.com; Arholma Södra Byväg 8; d from 700kr; 🅿🛜) hostel is here, too.

Finnhamn

Actually a congregation of islands, Finnhamn combines lush woods and meadows with sheltered coves, rocky cliffs and visiting eagle owls. It's a popular summertime spot, but there are enough quiet corners to indulge your inner hermit. Walking trails cover the island, delivering some awesome views. You can rent kayaks, canoes and SUPs at the kiosk at Paradisviken, in the middle of the island. Don't miss the top-notch restaurant, **Finnhamns Café & Krog** (☎08-54 24 62 12; www.finnhamn.se; Ingmarsö; lunch mains 145-165kr, dinner mains 165-285kr; ⏰11.30am-9pm Fri & Sat, to 4.30pm Sun May & Sep), known for its regional specialities and seafood. **STF Vandrarhem Utsikten** (☎08-54 24 62 12; www.finnhamn.se; 2-/3-/4-bed r 820/1050/1250kr, 2-/4-bed cabins 820/890kr, breakfast 100kr; ⏰year-round; @🛜) is the island's hostel.

Uppsala

Erken

Arholma

E4

77

280

Ekoln

Knivsta

Rimbo

Kapellskär

E18

77

Arlanda
Airport

Marö

Sigtuna

273

77

Furusund

Gräskö

Kudoxa

273

Ängsö
National
Park

Norröra

E4

Bergshamra

Xylan

Söderöra

268

276

Brunna

Siaröfortet
(Kyrkogårdsön)

Blidö

Svartlöga

Kungsängen

276

Östanå

Siarö

E18

Ljusterö

Finnhamn

Ängö

Mälaren

274

Ingmarsö

Svartsö

Stora
Kalholmen

Möja

Lidingö

Vaxholm

Grinda

Lökaön

Färingsö

Bromma
Airport

Fjäderholmarna

Gällnö

Vindö

Harö

Hasseludden

STOCKHOLM

Gustavsberg

Djurö

Eknö

Ekerö

Globen

Värmdö

Sandhamn

E20

Saltsjöbaden

222

Grönskär

Huddinge

Alta

Ingarö

Stavsnäs

Sandön

Botkyrka

Tyresö

Runmarö

Vårsta

Nämdö

Bullerö

Jordbro

Mörtö

Langviksskärs
naturreservat

257

Dalarö

Örnöboda

Årsta

Kymmendö

Havsbad

Ornö

Fiversättraön

Muskö

Fjärdlång

73

Ösmo

Gruvbryggan
(Gruvbyn)

Nynäshamn

Ränö

Utö

Bedarön

Älö

Nattarö

Himmerfjärden

N   0 ——————————— 40 km
    0 ——————————— 20 miles

Survival Guide

Riddarholmen (p39) GONCHAROVAIA/SHUTTERSTOCK ©

Before You Go

Book Your Stay

○ Expect high-quality accommodation in Stockholm, though it often comes with a hefty price tag.

○ Major hotel chains are invariably cheaper booked online and in advance; rates are also much cheaper in summer and at weekends.

○ Stockholm's Svenska Turistföreningen (STF) hostels are affiliated with Hostelling International (HI); a membership card yields a 50kr discount. Many have options for single, double and family rooms.

○ If things are busy in town, there are more than 20 hostels around the county easily reached by SL buses, trains or archipelago boats within an hour or so. There are also numerous summer campsites, many offering cheap cabin accommodation.

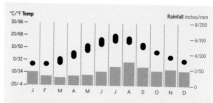

When to Go

Summer (mid-Jun–mid-Aug) Stockholm's long days, uncannily pretty light and mild weather are dreamy.

Winter (Dec–Feb) The city is a frosted cake, with holiday markets and mugs of *glögg* around every corner.

Autumn (Sep & Oct) Cooler weather, minimal crowds and beautiful autumn colours.

Useful Websites

c/o Stockholm (www. costockholm.com) Booking service for rooms and B&Bs.

Lonely Planet (www. lonelyplanet.com/ sweden/hotels) Accommodation recommendations.

Best Budget

Vandrarhem af Chapman & Skeppsholmen (www.stfchapman. com) Sleep on-board an antique ship at this popular hostel.

Långholmen Hotell & Vandrarhem (www. langholmen.com) Spend the night in the most comfortable prison cell you're likely to come across.

City Backpackers (www.citybackpackers. org) A fun place and the most central hostel in Stockholm.

City Hostel (www. cityhostel.se) A quiet night's rest on a budget, in Kungsholmen.

Hostel Bed & Breakfast (www.hostel bedandbreakfast.com) Informal spot with good facilities in a fun neighbourhood.

Best Midrange

Hobo Hotel (www.hobo.se) Hipster and fun, in a fantastic central location.

Hotel 'C' Stockholm (www.nordicchotel.com) Design hotel with great location and breakfast.

Hotel Anno 1647 (www.rexhotel.se) A charming historic hotel near Slussen.

Birger Jarl Hotel (www.birgerjarl.se) One of the city's original design hotels.

Rex Hotel (www.rexhotel.se) Small but stylish rooms and attractive common areas.

Best Top End

Grand Hôtel Stockholm (www.grandhotel.se) Iconic waterside luxury, where the glitterati stay.

Clarion Hotel Sign (www.clarionsign.com) Modern luxury hotel with cool design features.

Rival Hotel (www.rival.se) A retro boutique owned by one of the Bs from ABBA.

Hotel J (www.hotelj.com) This beautiful hotel makes it easy to pretend you own a yacht.

First Hotel Reisen (www.firsthotels.com) All the modern touches in an old town building.

Arriving in Stockholm

Stockholm Arlanda Airport

Arlanda Express (www.arlandaexpress.com; Centralstationen; one-way adult/youth 280/150kr) Trains between the airport and Centralstationen run every 10 to 15 minutes from 5am to 12.30am (less frequently after 9pm), taking 20 minutes.

Flygbussarna (www.flygbussarna.se; Cityterminalen) Buses to/from Cityterminalen leave from stop 11 in Terminal 5 every 10 to 15 minutes (adult/child one way 119/99kr, 40 minutes). Tickets can be purchased online, at Cityterminalen or at the Flygbuss self-service machine in Terminal 5.

Sverige Taxi (020-20 20 20; www.sverigetaxi.se), and **Taxi Stockholm** (15 00 00; www.taxistockholm.se) are reliable taxi services.

Getting Around

Tunnelbana (Metro)

◦ Stockholm's underground train system connects its various neighbourhoods; it's fast and efficient.

◦ There are three main lines: green, red and blue. Route maps are easy to navigate and posted at all stations.

◦ Trains generally run from 5am to 2.30am, but check schedules online.

Bus

◦ Inner-city buses radiate from Sergels Torg, Odenplan, Fridhemsplan (on Kungsholmen) and **Slussen**.

◦ Most buses run until midnight, but check schedules.

Tickets & Passes

o **Storstockholms Lokaltrafik** (SL; 08-600 10 00; www.sl.se; Centralstationen; ⏰7am-9pm) runs the tunnelbana (metro), local trains and buses.

o Buy tickets and passes at SL counters, ticket machines at tunnelbana stations, and Pressbyrå kiosks.

o The same tickets are valid on the tunnelbana, local trains and buses, and some local ferry routes.

o Single tickets are available, but if you're travelling more than once or twice it's better to get a refillable Access card.

o A single ticket costs 30kr-60kr and is valid for 75 minutes; it covers return trips and transfers between bus and metro.

o A 24-hour/72-hour/seven-day pass costs 120/240/315kr for an adult. Add another 20kr for a refillable Access card.

o Tickets cannot be bought on buses.

Bicycle

o Bicycles can be carried free on SL local trains as foldable 'hand luggage' only. They're not allowed in Centralstationen or on the tunnelbana.

o Self-service bicycle- and scooter-hire stands can be found across the city, such as Tier (www. tier.app) and Voi (www. voiscooters.com).

Taxi

o Taxis are readily available but fees are unregulated – check for a meter or arrange the fare first.

o Use one of the established, reputable firms, such as **Taxi Stockholm** (📞15 00 00; www.taxistockholm.se) or **Sverige Taxi** (📞020-20 20 20; www.sverigetaxi.se).

o The ridesharing company Uber (www. uber.com) also covers Stockholm.

Boat

o **Djurgårdsfärjan** city ferry services connect Gröna Lund Tivoli on Djurgården with Nybroplan (summer only) and Slussen (year-round) as frequently as every 10 minutes in summer; SL transport passes and tickets apply.

Tram

o The historic 7 tram runs between Norrmalmstorg and Skansen, passing most attractions on Djurgården.

o SL passes are valid.

Essential Information

Accessible Travel

o Stockholm is one of the easiest cities in which to travel around in a wheelchair.

o Some street crossings have ramps for wheelchairs and

Money-Saving Tips

o Book hotels and domestic travel online in advance. Summer rates are cheaper.

o Make lunch your main meal, as the locals do: look for *dagens rätt,* the daily lunch special, usually excellent value even at top-end restaurants (95kr–185kr).

Electricity

Type C
220V/50Hz

audio signals for visually impaired people, and many grocery stores are wheelchair accessible.

o People with disabilities will find transport services, ranging from trains to taxis, with adapted facilities.

o Public toilets and some hotel rooms have facilities for those with disabilities.

o Download Lonely Planet's free Accessible Travel guide from shop.lonelyplanet.com/categories/accessible-travel.com.

Business Hours

Except where indicated, we list hours for high season (mid-June to August). Expect more limited hours the rest of the year.

Banks 9.30am–3pm Monday to Friday; some city branches open to 5pm or 6pm

Bars & pubs 11am or noon to 1am or 2am

Government offices 9am–5pm Monday to Friday

Restaurants 11am–2pm and 5pm–10pm, often closed on Sunday and/or Monday, high-end restaurants often closed for a week or two in July or August

Shops 9am–6pm Monday to Friday, to 1pm Saturday

Discount Cards

A discount package called **Stockholm Pass** (☎08-663 00 80; www.stockholmpass.com; adult 1-/2-/3-/5-day pass 669/989/1209/1569kr, children roughly half-price) is offered by Go City and includes use of its hop-on, hop-off boats and buses, as well as admission to many attractions.

Emergency & Important Numbers

Ambulance	☎112
Fire department	☎112
Police	☎112
24-hour medical advice	☎1177
Non-emergency issues	☎113 13
Sweden's country code	☎46
International access code	☎00

Money

ATMs are plentiful, but many businesses in Stockholm are now cash-free and accept payment by credit or debit card only.

Forex-Vasagatan
(Centralplan 15; 🕑 5.30am-10pm Sun-Fri, to 6pm Sat; 🚇 T-Centralen) Near the tourist office and Centralstationen. There's also a branch in Terminal 2 at Arlanda airport.

Public Holidays

Midsummer brings life almost to a halt for three days: transport and other services are reduced, and most shops and smaller tourist offices close, as do some attractions.

Nyårsdag (New Year's Day) 1 January

Trettondedag Jul (Epiphany) 6 January

Långfredag, Påsk, Annandag Påsk (Good Friday, Easter Sunday and Monday) March/April

Första Maj (Labour Day) 1 May

Kristi Himmelsfärdsdag (Ascension Day) May/June

Pingst, Annandag Pingst (Whit Sunday and Monday) Late May or early June

Midsommardag (Midsummer's Day) Saturday between 19 and 25 June

Alla Helgons Dag (All Saints Day) Saturday, late October or early November

Juldag (Christmas Day) 25 December

Annandag Jul (Boxing Day) 26 December

Note also that Midsommarafton (Midsummer's Eve), Julafton (Christmas Eve; 24 December) and Nyårsafton (New Year's Eve; 31 December) are not official holidays but are generally nonworking days for most of the population.

Safe Travel

Pickpockets Watch your wallet in crowded, hectic places like Sergels torg and Centralstationen.

Taxi scams There's no fee regulation on taxis; check the price list posted in the taxi window and agree on a rate with the driver.

COVID-19 safety Be prepared to show proof of vaccination at indoor public events and wear a mask on crowded public transport. Anyone entering Sweden from a country outside of the Nordic region should take a PCR test if they experience symptoms of COVID-19 within 14 days of entering the country.

Taxes & Refunds

If you live outside the European Union (EU), you are entitled to a tax refund on your purchases. In Stockholm, Value Added Tax (VAT) is included in the price of items. When you buy something at a store displaying a Global Blue Tax-Free Shopping sticker, ask the cashier for a tax-free form. The goods must be in the original package, unused and unopened. Keep your receipts. Then display the form at the Global Blue counter at your last EU airport. This only applies to purchases of more than 200kr.

Telephone

◦ Smartphones are ubiquitous in Stockholm; coin-operated public telephones are virtually nonexistent.

Dos & Don'ts

o Smoking is banned in all bars, restaurants and hotels.

o Take off your shoes inside the front door when visiting a Swedish home.

o The most commonly uttered word in Swedish is *tack* – it means 'thanks'. Throw it out there!

o To call abroad from Sweden, dial zero and the country code. Within Sweden, dial the full area code including zero.

Mobile Phones

o The main providers are Tre, Telia, Comviq and Telenor.

o Buy local SIM cards from Pressbyrå locations, including at Arlanda Airport.

Phone Cards

o The few remaining payphones are operated with phonecards purchased from Pressbyrån newsagents (or with a credit card, although this is ludicrously expensive).

o Ask for a *telefon kort* for 50kr or 120kr, which roughly equate to 50 minutes and 120 minutes of local talk time, respectively. Be sure to specify you're using the card on a payphone, not refilling a mobile phone.

Toilets

Most public toilets charge 5kr or 10kr, payable with 5kr or 10kr coins or via SMS.

Tourist Information

Visit Stockholm
(☎ 08-508 28 508; www.visitstockholm.com; ⏲ telephone only 9am-6pm Mon-Fri, to 3pm Sat & Sun) The official visitors bureau has a regularly-updated website and is available for contact by phone.

Tours and Tickets
(☎ 076-196 92 33; www.stockholminfo.com; Stockholm Central Station, Centralplan 15; ⏲ 9am-7pm Mon-Fri, 10am-5pm Sat & Sun) Private tourism information outfit that books trips and tours,

also has brochures and information.

Royal Djurgården Visitor Center
(Map p74, C1; ☎ 08-667 77 01; www.royaldjurgarden.se; Djurgårdsvägen 2; ⏲ 9am-5pm daily; ☎ ; ☎ 7) With tourist information specific to Djurgården, this office at the edge of the Djurgården bridge is attached to Sjöcaféet, so you can grab a bite or a beverage as you plot your day.

Visas

o Citizens of EU countries can enter Sweden with a passport or a national identification card (passports are recommended) and stay indefinitely.

o Some nationalities will need a Schengen visa, good for 90 days.

o Non-EU passport holders from Australia, New Zealand, Canada and the US can enter and stay in Sweden without a visa for up to 90 days.

o Citizens of South Africa and many other African, Asian and some eastern European countries require tourist visas for entry to Sweden. These are only available in advance from Swedish embassies (allow two months). Visas are good for any 90 days within a six-month period.

o Migrationsverket (www.migrationsver ket.se) is the Swedish migration board and handles all applications for visas.

Responsible Travel

Allemansrätt

Sweden's Allemansrätt, or Right of Public Access, means everyone is free to roam in the countryside, collect berries and mushrooms, camp, hike, bike and swim (with the exception of private gardens, near homes and where crops are growing). Be sure to leave every place the way you found it.

Support local & give back

o Choose accommodation wisely. Most hotels and hostels are transparent about their sustainability efforts; look for Nordic Eco-labelled accommodation.

o Drink tap water and opt for locally grown, organic foods (labelled KRAV).

o Check your tour company's ecotourism standing with Nature's Best, which grades organisations based on strict sustainability criteria.

Leave a light footprint

o Avoid hiring a car – Stockholm has one of the world's best public transit systems, powered by 100% renewable energy.

o Better yet, commit to a human-powered visit: The compact city is delightful to walk, with a network of footpaths and green spaces. Or hire a kayak, bicycle, skateboard or electric scooter to get around. Bike-sharing programmes abound.

o Recycle. Stockholmers recycle everything; join them.

o Go vegan! Some of the best restaurants in the city specialise in vegan, raw, or vegetarian cuisine.

Language

Most Swedish sounds are similar to their English counterparts. One exception is *fh* (a breathy sound pronounced with rounded lips, like saying 'f' and 'w' at the same time), but with a little practice, you'll soon get it right. Note also that *ai* is pronounced as in 'aisle', *aw* as in 'saw', *air* as in 'hair', *eu* as the 'u' in 'nurse', *ew* as the 'ee' in 'see' with rounded lips, and *ey* as the 'e' in 'bet' but longer. Just read our pronunciation guides as if they were English and you'll be understood. The stressed syllables are indicated with italics.

Basics

Hello.
Hej.   hey

Goodbye.
Hej då.   hey daw

Yes.
Ja.   yaa

No.
Nej.   ney

Please.
Tack.   tak

Thank you (very much).
Tack (så mycket)   tak (saw *mew*·ke)

You're welcome.
Varsågod.   var·sha·*gohd*

Excuse me.
Ursäkta mig.   oor·*shek*·ta mey

Sorry.
Förlåt.   feur·*lawt*

How are you?
Hur mår du?   hoor mawr doo

Fine, thanks. And you?
Bra, tack. Och dig? braa tak o dey

What's your name?
Vad heter du?   vaad *hey*·ter doo

My name is ...
Jag heter ...   yaa *hey*·ter ...

Do you speak English?
Talar du engelska?
taa·lar doo *eng*·el·ska

I don't understand.
Jag förstår inte.
yaa feur·*shtawr in*·te

Eating & Drinking

What would you recommend?
Vad skulle ni rekommendera?
vaad *sku*·le nee re·ko·men·*dey*·ra

Do you have vegetarian food?
Har ni vegetarisk mat?
har nee ve·ge·*taa*·risk maat

I'll have ...
Jag vill ha ...   yaa vil haa ...

Cheers!
Skål!   skawl

I'd like (the) ...
Jag skulle vilja ha ...
yaa *sku*·le *vil*·yav haa ...

bill
räkningen   *reyk*·ning·en

drink list
dricklistan   *driks*·lis·tan

menu
menyn   me·*newn*

Emergencies

Help!
Hjälp!   yelp

Go away!
Försvinn!   feur·*shvin*

Call ...!
Ring ...! ring ...

a doctor
efter en doktor ef·ter en dok·tor

the police
polisen poh·lee·sen

I'm lost.
Jag har gått vilse. yaa har got vil·se

I'm sick.
Jag är sjuk. yaa air fhook

Where are the toilets?
Var är toaletten?
var air toh·aa·le·ten

Transport & Directions

Where's the ...?
Var ligger ...? var li·ger ...

bank
banken ban·ken

post office
posten pos·ten

tourist office
turistinformationen
too·rist·in·for ma·fhoh·nen

I'd like one ... (to Stockholm) please.
Jag skulle vilja ha en ... (till Stockholm).
yaa sku·le vil·ya haa eyn ... (til stok·holm)

one-way ticket
enkelbiljett en·kel·bil·yet

return ticket
returbiljett re·toor·bil·yet

What time does the train/bus leave?
När avgår tåget/bussen?
nair aav·gawr taw·get/bu·sen

Can you stop here?
Kan du stanna här?
kan doo sta·na hair

Shopping & Services

I'm looking for ...
Jag letar efter ... yaa ley·tar ef·ter ...

How much is it?
Hur mycket kostar det?
hoor mew·ke kos·tar de

Time & Numbers

What time is it?
Hur mycket är klockan?
hur mew·ke air klo·kan

It's (two) o'clock.
Klockan är (två). klo·kan air (tvaw)

in the morning
på förmiddagen
paw feur·mi·daa·gen

in the afternoon
på eftermiddagen
paw ef·ter·mi·daa·gen

yesterday
igår ee·gawr

tomorrow
imorgon ee·mor·ron

1	*ett*	et
2	*två*	tvaw
3	*tre*	trey
4	*fyra*	few·ra
5	*fem*	fem
6	*sex*	seks
7	*sju*	fhoo
8	*åtta*	o·ta
9	*nio*	nee·oh
10	*tio*	tee·oh
100	*ett hundra*	et hun·dra
1000	*ett tusen*	et too·sen

Behind the Scenes

Send Us Your Feedback

We love to hear from travellers – your comments help make our books better. We read every word, and we guarantee that your feedback goes straight to the authors. Visit **lonelyplanet.com/contact** to submit your updates and suggestions.

Note: We may edit, reproduce and incorporate your comments in Lonely Planet products such as guidebooks, websites and digital products, so let us know if you don't want your comments reproduced or your name acknowledged. For a copy of our privacy policy visit lonelyplanet.com/privacy.

Becky's Thanks

Thanks to my mom, Christina, for rounding up a bunch of extra info from her friends; Paul Smith for inspiring the pinball quest; James Borup for the brewery intel; the Auld Dub in general; and all the various editors in-house at Lonely Planet for helping whip the resulting content into shape.

Acknowledgements

Cover photographs: (front): Interior of the Stockholm City Hall, Pink-Badger/Getty Images ©; (back) Old town of Stockholm, leoks/Shutterstock ©

Photographs pp28–9 (clockwise from bottom left): b-hide the scene/Shutterstock ©, Viacheslav Savitskiy/Shutterstock ©, Gelia/Getty Images ©

This Book

This 5th edition of Lonely Planet's *Pocket Stockholm* guidebook was researched and written by Becky Ohlsen and curated by Charles Rawlings-Way. The previous edition was also written by Becky and curated by Charles. This guidebook was produced by the following:

Destination Editor
Gemma Graham

Senior Product Editor
Sandie Kestell

Product Editor
Hannah Cartmel

Cartographer
Corey Hutchison

Book Designer
Hannah Blackie

Assisting Editors Janet Austin, Chris Pitts

Cover Researchers Gwen Cotter, Naomi Parker

Thanks to Jenna Myers, Ambika Shree

Index

See also separate subindexes for:

⊗ **Eating p152**

⊜ **Drinking p153**

✪ **Entertainment p153**

⊜ **Shopping p153**

SORINA CHIRITA

LONELY PLANET IN THE WILD